The Oneness and Simplicity of God

The
Oneness and Simplicity
of God

Barry D. Smith

☙PICKWICK *Publications* • Eugene, Oregon

THE ONENESS AND SIMPLICITY OF GOD

Copyright © 2014 Barry D. Smith. All rights reserved. Except for brief quotations in critical publications or reviews, no part of this book may be reproduced in any manner without prior written permission from the publisher. Write: Permissions, Wipf and Stock Publishers, 199 W. 8th Ave., Suite 3, Eugene, OR 97401.

Pickwick Publications
An Imprint of Wipf and Stock Publishers
199 W. 8th Ave., Suite 3
Eugene, OR 97401

www.wipfandstock.com

ISBN 13: 978-1-62564-125-0

Cataloguing-in-Publication data:

Smith, Barry D., 1957 December 4–

The oneness and simplicity of God / Barry D. Smith.

xvi + 138 pp. ; 23 cm. Includes bibliographical references.

ISBN 13: 978-1-62564-125-0

1. God—Simplicity. 2. God—Attributes. 3. God (Christianity)—History of doctrines. I. Title.

BT148 S58 2014

Manufactured in the U.S.A.

CONTENTS

Introduction | vii
List of Abbreviations | ix

1. God as Numerically One | 1
2. From God as Numerically One to God as Simple | 23
3. Traditional Argumentation for the Simplicity Doctrine | 56
4. Recent Defense of the Simplicity Doctrine | 84
5. Concluding Summary and Evaluation | 120

Bibliography | 131

Introduction

THAT YHWH IS NUMERICALLY one is a fundamental assertion of the Hebrew Bible. Building on this, Christian theologians affirm that God has another, more fundamental type of oneness. God is one not merely in the sense of being the one and only God, but also in the sense of being simple or non-composite, having no parts of any kind. The most obvious type of composition that God lacks is that resulting from having or being a body. Other, less obvious types of composition are also denied of God, what can be called instances of metaphysical compositeness. Two unusual implications follow from the simplicity doctrine. First, since God is simple, there can be no distinction between God and any one of God's properties or even between God and all of God's properties, which is known as property-deity identification. The second unusual implication of the simplicity doctrine is that each of God's attributes is the same as all the others, so that each attribute denotes every other attribute, what is known as property-property identity. The simplicity doctrine has been maintained for centuries by Christian theologians without any hint that it is mistaken or meaningless. Not until the modern period was its validity questioned.

The purpose of this monograph is to examine the simplicity doctrine, in order to determine whether indeed Christians should think of God as simple. Traditionally, there have been two types of arguments used to support it. First, scriptural support is adduced: theologians look for statements in the Bible from which God's simplicity can be inferred. Second, it is argued that the nature of God is such that God cannot be other than simple: to conceive God as composite in any respect is logically contradictory. It is the conclusion of this investigation, however, that neither type of argument provides any reason to accept the simplicity doctrine. A relatively recent assault on the coherency of doctrine of divine simplicity has come from

Introduction

Alvin Plantinga. His work *Does God Have a Nature?* has generated many responses from those who propose to preserve some version of simplicity doctrine. The effect of his work has been to initiate new defenses of the doctrine. These recent attempts to argue for the coherence and validity of the simplicity doctrine must likewise be judged to be unsuccessful.

The final conclusion reached in this monograph is that there is no basis for ascribing simplicity to God. The idea is not biblical, but originates in Greek philosophy and has been unduly introduced into Christian theology. Although generally it is a good theological methodology to respect church tradition and not dismiss it out of hand too readily, in the case of the simplicity doctrine it would seem that the church has made a mistake. To claim that God's mode of being is that of simplicity is to exceed the limits of human knowledge. It should not be thought, however, that denying that God is simple means that God therefore must be must a composite being, having a set of God-making properties. Rather, it is argued that even to ask whether God is simple or composite is disallowed. In other words, the question of how God has attributes, or exemplifies properties, is a pseudo-question, the answering of which can only result in transcendental illusion. An apophatic theological methodology is to be preferred.

Abbreviations

1 Bar.	*First Baruch*
1 En.	*First Enoch*

Alcinous

Didask. *Didaskalikos (Handbook of Platonism)*

Ambrose

De fide *De fide ad Gratianum Augustum (Exposition of the Christian Faith)*

Anselm

Monol. *Monologium*
Prosl. *Proslogium*

Appian

Syr. *Syriaca*

Aristotle

Eth. Eud. *Eudemian Ethics*
Metaph. *Metaphysics*
Phys. *Physics*

Arnobius

Adv. nat. *Adversus Nationes (Against the Pagans)*

Abbreviations

Athanasius

Adv. gent.	*Oratio contra gentes (Against the Nations)*
Ar.	*Orationes contra Arianos (Orations against the Arians)*
De syn.	*De synodis Arimini in Italia et Seleuciae (On the Synods of Ariminum and Seleucia)*
Decr.	*De decretis Nicaenae synodi (On the Council of Nicaea)*
Ep. Afr.	*Epistula ad Afros (Letter to the Bishops of Africa)*

Athenagoras

Leg.	*Legatio pro Christianis (A Plea for Christians)*

Augustine

Civ. Dei	*De civitate Dei (On the City of God)*
Conf.	*Confessiones (Confessions)*
De Trin.	*De trinitate (On the Trinity)*
Fide et symb.	*De fide et symbolo (Of Faith and the Creed)*

Basil

Adv. Eunom.	*Adversus Eunomium (Against Eunomius)*
Ep.	*Epistolae (Letters)*

Boethius

De Hebd.	*De Hebdomadibus*
Trin.	*De Trinitate (On the Trinity)*

Bonaventure

Comm. sent.	*Commentaria in quatuor libros sententiarum (Commentary on the Four Books of Sentences)*

Cicero

Acad.	*Academica*

Abbreviations

Clement of Alexandria
Strom.   *Stromata (Miscellanies)*

Clement of Rome
1 Clem.   *First Clement*
2 Clem.   *Second Clement*

Cyril of Alexandria
De Trin.   *De Sancta Trinitate (On the Holy Trinity)*

Cyril of Jerusalem
Cat. lect.   *Catechetical Lecture*

Didymus of Alexandria
De spir. sancto   *De spiritu sancto (On the Holy Spirit)*

Diod.   *Diodorus Siculus*

Ep. Arist.   *Letter of Aristeas*

Eusebius
Praep. ev.   *Praeparatio evangelica (Preparation for the Gospel)*

Friedrich Schleiermacher
CF   *The Christian Faith*

Gregory Nazianzus
Or.   *Oration*

Gregory of Nyssa
Abl.   *Ad Ablabium. Quod non sint tres dei (On Not Three Gods)*
Con. Eunom.   *Contra Eunomium (Against Eunomius)*
In eccl.   *In ecclesiasten homiliae (Homilies on Ecclesiastes)*
Or. cat.   *Oratio catechetica magna (The Great Catechism)*

Abbreviations

Hilary
De Trin.	*De Trinitate (On the Trinity)*
Hippol.	*Hippolytus*

Immanuel Kant
PR	*Critique of Pure Reason*

Irenaeus
Adv. haer.	*Adversus haereses (Against Heresies)*

John Chrysostom
De incomp.	*De incomprehensibili Dei natura (On the Incomprehensible Nature of God)*

John Duns Scotus
DPP	*Tractatus de primo principio (Treatise on the First Principle)*
Ord.	*Ordinatio or Opus Oxoniense (Oxford Lectures)*

John Locke
Ess.	*Essay Concerning Human Understanding*

John of Damascus
O.F.	*An Exact Exposition of the Orthodox Faith*

John Owen
Vind.	*Vindiciae Evangelicae*

Josephus
Ant.	*Antiquities of the Jews*
War	*The Jewish War*

Jub.	*Book of Jubilees*

Justin Martyr

1 Apol.	*First Apology*
2 Apol.	*Second Apology*
Dial.	*Dialogue with Trypho*

Karl Barth

CD	*Church Dogmatics*

Lactantius

D.I.	*Divinarum institutionum (Divine Institutes)*

Maximus Confessor

Cent. gnost.	*Centuria gnostica (Chapters on Knowledge)*

Minucius Felix

Oct.	*Octavius*

Novatian

De Trin.	*De Trinitate (On the Trinity)*

Origen

Con. Cels.	*Contra Celsum (Against Celsus)*
Comm. Jn.	*Commentaria in Evangelium Joannem (Commentary on John)*
Prin.	*De principiis (On First Principles)*

Peter Lombard

Sent.	*Sententiae (Sentences)*

Philo

Contempl.	*De Vita Contemplativa (The Contemplative Life)*
Deus	*Quod Deus sit immutabilis (That God is Unchangeable)*
Exod.	*Exodus*

Abbreviations

Fug.	*De Fuga et Inventione (Flight and Finding)*
Her.	*Quis rerum divinarum heres sit (Who is the Heir?)*
Leg.	*Legum allegoriae (Allegorical Interpretation)*
Migr.	*De Migratione Abrahami (On the Migration of Abraham)*
Opif.	*De opificio mundi (On the Creation of the World)*
Post.	*De posteritate Caini (On the Posterity of Cain)*
Praem.	*De praemiis et poenis (On Rewards and Punishments)*
Sobr.	*De Sobrietate (Sobriety)*
Somn.	*De somniis (On Dreams)*
Spec.	*De specialibus legibus (On the Special Laws)*

Plato

Parm.	*Parmenides*
Phaed.	*Phaedrus*
Rep.	*Republic*
Soph.	*Sophist*
Tim.	*Timaeus*

Plotinus

Enn.	*Enneads*

Plutarch

De E.	*De e apud Delphos (On the E at Delphi)*
Def. or.	*De defectu oraculorum (On the Failure of Oracles)*
Is.	*De Iside et Osiride (Isis and Osiris)*

Paul Tillich

ST	*Systematic Theology*

Polyb.	*Polybius*

Proclus
Instit. theol.   *Institutia theologica (Elements of Theology)*

Pseudo-Dionysius
De div. nom.   *De divinis nominibus (On Divine Names)*

Seneca
Epist.   *Epistles*

Shepherd of Hermas
Man.   *Mandates*
Vis.   *Visions*

Sib. Or.   *Sibylline Oracles*

Tacitus
Hist.   *Historiae (Histories)*

Tatian
Or.   *Oratio ad Graecos (Address to the Greeks)*

Tertullian
Ad. nat.   *Ad nationes (To the Nations)*
Adv. Marc.   *Adversus Marcionem (Against Marcion)*
Apol.   *Apologeticus pro christianis (Apology for the Christians)*
De virg. vel.   *De virginibus velandis (On Veiling Virgins)*

Theophilus of Antioch
Ad Autol.   *Apologia Ad Autolycum*

Thomas Aquinas
Compend.   *Compendium theologiae*
De ent. et ess.   *De ente et essentia*

De potent.	*De potentia*
De ver.	*Quaestiones disputatae de veritate*
SCG	*Summa contra gentiles*
Sent.	*Scriptum super libros sententiarum (Commentary on the Sentences)*
ST	*Summa theologiae*

1

God as Numerically One

God as One in the Hebrew Bible

IN THE ANCIENT WORLD divinity is plural; the various aspects of human experience are distributed among many gods. Contrary to this polytheistic presupposition, Israel is to confess that YHWH is numerically one, which means there is no God but YHWH.[1] For this reason, unlike the nation's many neighboring peoples, Israelite religion does not have a pantheon of gods.[2] The confession that YHWH is numerically one is the confession that YHWH is unique, not just one being among many beings of the same type, not even the greatest among them. In addition, it requires the rejection of a feminine counterpart to YHWH. It seems that human beings assume that the duality of masculine and feminine must extend to the divine since it is so fundamental to human experience.[3] This confession that YHWH is

1. At times what is said about YHWH might lead one to think that he is only one of many gods. There are, for example, hymns in the Old Testament in which YHWH is extolled as greatest among the gods (Exod 15:11; Pss 95:3; 97:9), from which one may infer that there is more than one God. When all data are taken into account, however, it is clear that the Hebrew Bible affirms a theoretical monotheism, as opposed to simply asserting YHWH's supremacy or imposing on the Israelites the requirement of practical monolatry.

2. The fact that YHWH functions as a proper name should not be taken to mean that there is only one God named YHWH, but rather that YHWH alone is God. A polytheist would agree that YHWH is one in the former sense, but would admit other "ones" as gods as members of a pantheon. See Clements, *Old Testament Theology*, 72–78.

3. In Canaanite religion, as evidenced in twelfth-century BCE Ugaritic texts from Ras

The Oneness and Simplicity of God

numerically one also includes the idea that YHWH himself is not divisible into many, quasi-independent YHWH's.[4] In spite of the apodictic certainty with which it is asserted in Scripture, the Israelites nevertheless struggled to maintain a theoretical monotheism; only after the exile, did it become a fixture of their national religious consciousness.[5] In the Hebrew Bible no

---

Shamra, the supreme God El, the father of other gods, human beings, and all creatures, has Asherah (or Athirat) as his feminine counterpart. Her full title is Lady Asharah (or Athirat) of the Sea. It is probable that, contrary to the declaration of the Shema, the pre-exilic Israelites considered the goddess Asherah to be YHWH's consort. Evidence for this comes from references to the goddess Asherah and not to a wooden cult object (1 Kgs 15:13; 18:19; 2 Kgs 23:4–7; 2 Chr 15:16) (Olyan, *Asherah and the Cult of YHWH in Israel*; Smith, *The Early History of God: YHWH and the Other Deities in Ancient Israel*; Binger, *Asherah: Goddesses in Ugarit, Israel and the Old Testament*). Not surprisingly figurines that are probably images of Asherah dating from the eighth and early seventh centuries are common archaeological finds (Kletter, *The Judean Pillar-Figurines and the Archaeology of Asherah*; Hadley, *The Cult of Asherah in Ancient Israel and Judah: Evidence for a Hebrew Goddess*; Dever, *Did God Have a Wife? Archaeology and Folk Religion in Ancient Israel*). An idol of Asherah was frequently found in Solomon's Temple during its history (Patai, *The Hebrew Goddess*, 50). Manasseh, for example, was condemned for introducing an Asherah into the Temple (2 Kgs 21:7). In addition, inscriptions linking YHWH and Asherah have been discovered recently (Freedman, "YHWH of Samaria and His Asherah"; Hadley, *The Cult of Asherah in Ancient Israel and Judah*, 86–102; Van der Toorn, "Goddesses in Early Israelite Religion," 89). At Kuntillet Arjud in the Sinai desert, an inscription on a piece of pottery reads "I have blessed you by YHWH of Samaria and his Asherah," while two other inscriptions from the same site read "I bless you by YHWH of Teman and his Asherah." Similarly, in another inscription found at Khirbet el-Kom near Hebron YHWH and Asherah are again associated: "Blessed be Uriyahu by YHWH and by his Asherah; from his enemies he saved him." In these cases, it is probable that the goddess Asherah is the female consort of YHWH.

4. The proper name Baal denotes a Canaanite nature-fertility and storm god, who is a son of El (see the Baal cycle found in the Ugartic texts). There are, however, several, quasi-independent Baals distinguished from one another by qualifying epithets. Sometimes Baal is connected with a place, such as Peor (Num 25:3), Gad (Josh 11:17), Hermon (Judg 3:3), and Hamon (Song 8:11). There is also a reference to Baal of the covenant (Judg 8:33; 9:4) and Baal Zebub (flies or prince) (2 Kgs 1:2, 3, 6, 16). The god Baal becomes in human experience many Baals.

5. In the second century BCE, pro-Hellenistic Jews rededicate the Jerusalem Temple to the Olympic Zeus (Dios Olympiou), but this seems to be not so much a reversion to polytheism as an identification of YHWH with the Greek god Zeus (4Q386 frag. 1, cols. 2–3; 1 Macc 1:29–64; 2 Macc 5:24—26:11; Josephus, *Ant.* 12.5.4; 248–56; *War* 1.1.2; 34–35; see Polyb. 28.18.1–23.5; 29.27.1–8; Diod. 31.2; Appian, *Syr.*, 66; Justinus, 34.3.1–3; Livy 45.12.1–8; Tacitus, *Hist.* 5.5). Tacitus writes about the Jewish understanding of God: "The Egyptians worship many animals and images of monstrous form; the Jews have purely mental conceptions of Deity, *as one in essence*. They call those profane who make representations of God in human shape out of perishable materials. They believe that being to be supreme and eternal, neither capable of representation, nor of decay. They therefore do not allow any images to stand in their cities, much less in their temples. This

theoretical argumentation is provided for the belief that YHWH is the one and only God; rather the evidence cited as warrant for it is experiential: YHWH's incomparable power as experienced by Israel and other peoples.

The Shema (Deut 6:4)

The *textus classicus* for God's numerical oneness is the Shema: "Hear Israel, YHWH our God YHWH one" (שמע ישראל יהוה אלהינו יהוה אחד) (Deut 6:4).[6] The Shema begins with a vocative address ("Hear, Israel"), and is followed by four nominative elements: the divine name (YHWH) twice, a noun with a pronominal suffix ("our God") and a numeral ("one").[7] This passage has presented exegetes with several difficulties. Grammatically these six words could be interpreted in different ways: "Hear, Israel: YHWH is our God, YHWH alone"; "Hear, Israel: YHWH our God is one YHWH"; "Hear, Israel: YHWH is our God; YHWH is one"; or "Hear, Israel: YHWH our God, YHWH is one." In the first interpretation, the word "one" (אחד) functions as an adverb and has the meaning of "alone."[8] On this reading, the Shema is not a statement about YHWH, but rather one about Israel's covenantal obligation to have no other God than YHWH. The more common expression for "alone," however, is לבד (see 2 Kgs 19:15, 19 and Ps 86:10).[9] Another problem with this translation is that syntactically it interprets "our God" as a predicate nominative ("YHWH *is* our God"). While this interpretation is not impossible (see 2 Chr 13:10), given its frequency in Deuteronomy, it is more probable that the phrase "YHWH our God" is formulaic, functioning as the subject.[10] The second

---

flattery is not paid to their kings, nor this honour to our Emperors" (*Hist.* 5.8).

6. Peter Lombard finds proof of the unity of God in the Song of Moses (Exod 15:3): "In the Canticle in Exodus there is also read: 'The Lord, Omnipotent (is) his name'; it does not say the Lords, wanting to signify the unity" (*Sent.* I. 2.4). The fact that there is said to be only one "Lord" (*Dominus*) proves the unity (*unitas*) of God. Lombard does not recognize, however, that the word "Lord" (*dominus*) is actually a translation of the proper name YHWH and so grammatically cannot be made plural.

7. See Bavinck, *Reformed Dogmatics*, vol. 2, *God and Creation*, 170–73.

8. See McBride, "The Yoke of the Kingdom: An Exposition of Deuteronomy 6:4–5."

9. Josh 22:20; 2 Sam 7:23; 1 Kgs 4:19; 1 Chr 29:1; Job 23:13; 31:15; Song 6:9; Isa 51:2; Ezek 33:24; 37:22; Zech 14:9 are proposed as examples of the use of אחד with the meaning of "alone." See the discussion in Block, "How Many is God? An Investigation into the Meaning of Deuteronomy 6:4–5," 199–200.

10. יהוה + אלהים with a suffix is never a subject-predicate in its more than 300

possible interpretation, "YHWH our God is one YHWH," asserts that there is only one YHWH, in the sense that there is only one God named YHWH. This might be necessary if there were many geographical locations with which YHWH was associated, in which case a *de facto* poly-Yahwism might develop.[11] This interpretation, however, seems unusual and unexpected in the context of Deut 6. It is probable that the intention of Deut 6:4 is to assert the numerical oneness of YHWH, in which case either interpretation three or four would be the best.[12] The question now is to determine whether the last four words compose one nominal clause or two. If two nominal clauses, then "our God" is a predicate nominative, which as already indicated is improbable. This leaves the option of one nominal clause. On this interpretation, "our God" is not a predicate nominative, but stands in apposition to YHWH; the second YHWH is not superfluous since it is repeated for emphasis: "Hear, Israel: YHWH our God, YHWH is one."[13]

An eschatological midrash on Deut 6:4 is found in the book of Zechariah. It is prophesied that, after their attack on Jerusalem, the nations will be destroyed by divine intervention, which represents the final triumph of God (Zech 12–14).[14] In the context of the eschatological defeat of the enemies of Jerusalem, it said that at that time "YHWH will be king over all the earth" (14:9a).[15] In this passage, earth must mean the whole world, not just Palestine. Before this day Israel has confessed that YHWH reigns as king in principle (Pss 93:1; 97:1; 99:1); after this day, however, YHWH will

---

occurrences in Deuteronomy. See also Exod 20:12; Hos 12:10; 13:4; Isa 26:13; Jer 14:22.

11. YHWH is associated with Sinai (Deut 33:2; Judg 5:5; Ps 68:8), Paran (Deut 33:2; Hab 3:3), Seir/Edom (Judg 5:4), and Teman (Hab 3:3).

12. See the similar use of "one" in Job 23:13; Ezek 37:17; Song 6:9; Zech 14:7. It is sometimes argued that in nominative clauses of classification, as "YHWH is one" (יהוה אחד) would be, the word order is predicate-subject (Andersen, *The Hebrew Verbless Clause in the Pentateuch*, 42–45) (Andersen's Rule #3). As Waltke and O'Connor note, however, the use of a numeral as a predicate seems "to neutralize the word-order patterns" (*An Introduction to Biblical Hebrew Syntax*, 134). Support for this interpretation is found in the New Testament citation of Deut 6:4 κύριος ὁ θεὸς ἡμῶν κύριος εἷς ἐστιν (Mark 12:29–30), which is identical to the LXX. The Nash Papyrus likewise supports this interpretation: יהוה אלהינו יהוה אחד הוא. Although perhaps tenuous, one could argue that the nominative clause is one of identification since only God is (the) one, in which case the word order subject-predicate would be correct.

13. In this case the phrase "YHWH our God" is a nominative absolute, also known as *casus pendens*. See Exod 34:6 "YHWH, YHWH, God compassionate," etc.

14. Meyers and Meyers, *Zechariah 9–14*, 438–40; Klein, *Zechariah*, 412–13; Petersen, *Zechariah 9–14 and Malachi*, 147–49.

15. והיה יהוה למלך על־כל־הארץ

be king in actuality. As a result of being king, YHWH will be confessed as the one and only God: "In that day YHWH will be one, and his name one" (14:9b).¹⁶ The two coordinate clauses are in synthetic parallelism, in which case "YHWH" is the equivalent of "his name" (see Lev 24:11).¹⁷ Whereas God is confessed as numerically one in the Shema by the Israelites, in the eschatological future YHWH will be universally acknowledged as the one true God; implicit is the rejection of plurality in the divine.¹⁸ YHWH is not now king or acknowledged as the only God, but shall be.¹⁹

YHWH as the One and Only God

That YHWH is numerically one is expressed in the Hebrew Bible frequently and in different ways. In the Song of the Sea, it is asked, "Who is like you among the gods (מי כמכה באלם), YHWH? Who is like you (מי כמכה), majestic in holiness, awesome in praises, working wonders? (Exod 15:11).²⁰ The implication is that YHWH is not classifiable as one of the gods. What distinguishes YHWH in human experience from the gods of the nations is his incomparable power: no other god has done what YHWH has done.²¹ Similarly, in the Song of Moses, after describing how the gods of Israel's enemies failed to help them, the author has YHWH assert, "See now that I,

---

16. ביום ההוא יהיה יהוה אחד ושמו אחד

17. See the parallels in Mal 1:11: "'My name will be great among the nations, and in every place incense is going to be offered to my name, and a grain offering that is pure; for my name will be great among the nations', says YHWH of hosts"; Zeph 3:9: "For then I will give to the peoples purified lips, that all of them may call on the name of YHWH, to serve him shoulder to shoulder"; and Jer 3:17: "At that time they will call Jerusalem 'The throne of YHWH', and all the nations will be gathered to it, to Jerusalem, for the name of YHWH; nor will they walk anymore after the stubbornness of their evil heart."

18. As stated in Zech 13:2, "'It will come about in that day', declares YHWH of hosts, 'that I will cut off the names of the idols from the land, and they will no longer be remembered; and I will also remove the prophets and the unclean spirit from the land.'"

19. See the connection made between Zech 14:9 and Deut 6:4 in the early rabbinic text *Sipre Deuteronomy*. The apparent redundancy of the second reference to YHWH is said to have midrashic significance (31). The phrase "YHWH, our God" refers to the fact that YHWH is God of the children of Israel in this world, whereas the second phrase "YHWH is one" refers to the fact that in the world to come YHWH will be God of all creatures of the world, including gentiles. Zech 14:9 is then cited as a proof-text.

20. Childs, *The Book of Exodus*, 240–53.

21. See Exod 7:4; 8:10; 9:14; 13:9, 14; 14:31; 18:11; 34:10; Deut 3:24; 9:29; 10:21; 11:2-3; 20:1; 32:31; Josh 2:10–11; 3:10; 4:23–24; 2 Sam 7:23; Ps 86:8; 89:6; 113:5; see Isa 64:4.

The Oneness and Simplicity of God

I am he, and there is no god with me" (Deut 32:39).[22] The two statements are in synthetic parallelism: "I, I am he" means idiomatically that there is no other god with YHWH in the sense of being equal to him.[23] Implicitly this is the reason why the gods of Israel's enemies did not rise up and help them: they are not the true God. As YHWH rhetorically asks, "Where are their gods, the rock in which they sought refuge?" (Deut 32:37).[24] Along the same lines, in Deut 3:24 Moses prays, "O Adonai YHWH, you have begun to show your servant your greatness and your strong hand; for what god is there in heaven or on earth who can do such works and mighty acts as yours?" YHWH is unique among the gods because of his unrivaled acts. Likewise, because of his manifest greatness YHWH is described as supreme among the gods: "For YHWH your God is the God of gods (אלהי האלהים) and the lord of lords, the great, the mighty and awesome God" (Deut 10:17).[25] What is meant is by the phrase "God of gods" is that, whatever they are, the other gods are not the same as YHWH. Finally, in Deut 4:35, it is affirmed, "YHWH, he is God; there is no other apart from him."[26] The warrant cited for this confession is the Israelites's experience of YHWH's unparalleled acts in the Exodus and at Mt. Sinai (see Exod 6:6; 7:3; 12:30–36; 14:4; 15:3; 19:17–20; 20:18–19; 24:15–18).[27] The major premise of the argument is that only the *true* God can do such things.[28]

22. אני אני הוא ואין אלהים עמדי

23. A similar statement is found in 2 Sam 7:28 "And now Adonai YHWH, you are he" (ועתה אדני יהוה אתה־הוא) and Isa 37:16 "You are he" (אתה־הוא).

24. See Exod 8:9–10: Moses said to Pharaoh, "The honor is yours to tell me: when shall I entreat for you and your servants and your people, that the frogs be destroyed from you and your houses, that they may be left only in the Nile? Then he said, 'Tomorrow'. So he said, 'May it be according to your word, *that you may know that there is no one like YHWH our God*.'"

25. Jethro, Moses' father-in-law, concedes that YHWH is greater than the other gods based on the events of the Exodus (Exod 18:10–11).

26. יהוה הוא האלהים אין עוד מלבדו

27. Deut 4:33–34: "Has any people heard the voice of God speaking from the midst of the fire, as you have heard it, and survived? Or has a god tried to go to take for himself a nation from within another nation by trials, by signs and wonders and by war and by a mighty hand and by an outstretched arm and by great terrors, as YHWH your God did for you in Egypt before your eyes?" See also Deut 6:22; 7:19; 11:2–3; 26:8.

28. Driver, *Deuteronomy*, 75–77; Craigie, *The Book of Deuteronomy*, 141–44; Hall, *Deuteronomy*, 105–9. For the Israelites, there are two primary sources of knowledge of YHWH, their God: the exodus and Sinai. Such knowledge is empirical, based on the principle of sufficient causation: an effect must be commensurate with its cause, or for every fact F, there must be an explanation why F is the case.

Whatever they really are, the other gods are not the true God since they cannot produce the effects that the true God can (Deut 4:32–34). A few verses later the formula "there is no other" (אֵין עוֹד) appears: "YHWH, he is God in heaven above and on the earth below; there is no other" (Deut 4:39).[29] For YHWH to be God in heaven and earth explains why there is no other god: YHWH has no rival anywhere because he is God everywhere.

In his prayer of thanksgiving, upon hearing about YHWH's dynastic promise to him, David confesses, "For there is none like you, and there is no God except you" (2 Sam 7:22).[30] His confession is that YHWH is unique or incomparable ("none like you"), from which it follows that YHWH alone is God ("no God except you"). It is not that YHWH is one god among many, not even the greatest of them, but rather that YHWH is the only true God. YHWH's incomparability in relation to the gods is parallel to Israel's incomparability in relation to the nations (2 Sam 7:23). The narrative of Elijah's contest with the 450 prophets of Baal and 400 prophets of Asherah on Mount Carmel is likewise intended to prove the unreality of the other gods, in particular Baal, who could effect nothing in spite of many inducements by his prophets (1 Kgs 18:17–40). Similarly, because of his unprecedented healing from leprosy, Naaman confesses that YHWH alone is God: "Now I know that there is no God in all the earth but in Israel" (2 Kgs 5:15; see 2 Kgs 19:15).[31] The confession that YHWH alone is God, in spite of the fact that human beings believe in many other gods, occurs in Solomon's prayer of dedication of the Temple (1 Kgs 8). The request is made that YHWH would maintain his covenantal faithfulness in order that the nations would recognize that YHWH alone is God: "In order that all the peoples of the earth may know that YHWH is God; there is no other" (1 Kgs 8:59–60) (see also 1 Kgs 20:23, 28).[32] The assumption is that only the true God can so act in human history.[33]

In the invocation of his prayer, Hezekiah confesses that YHWH is the one and only God: "YHWH, the God of Israel, enthroned among the cherubim, you are God, you alone" (2 Kgs 19:15; see Isa 37:16, 20).[34] The Assyr-

29. יהוה הוא האלהים בשמים ממעל ועל־ארץ מתחת אין עוד
30. אין כמוך אין אלהים זולתך
31. אין אלהים בכל־הארץ כי אם־בישראל. See Cogan and Tadmor, *II Kings*, 67.
32. למען דעת כל־עמי הארץ כי יהוה הוא האלהים אין עוד

33. See 1 Kgs 8:23: "There is no God like you in heaven above or on earth beneath, keeping covenant and showing lovingkindness to your servants who walk before you with all their heart."

34. יהוה אלהי ישראל ישב הכרבים אתה־הוא האלהים לבדך. On cherubim see Gen 3:24; Exod 25:18–20.

The Oneness and Simplicity of God

ians were able to conquer the other nations because their gods were merely idols, the work of men's hands, gods of wood and stone (2 Kgs 19:17–18).[35] By contrast, YHWH is said to be the "living God" (אלהים חי), by which is meant the true and therefore powerful God, as opposed to those ineffectual idols (2 Kgs 19:16).[36] It is on this basis that Hezekiah in the supplication of his prayer petitions YHWH to protect his kingdom from the Assyrian invaders, even appealing to YHWH's self-interest. Hezekiah says, "Now, YHWH, our God, deliver us from his hand, in order that all the kingdoms of the earth may know that you alone, YHWH, are God" (2 Kgs 19:19).[37]

In his penitential prayer, Nehemiah begins by confessing YHWH's uniqueness: "You alone are YHWH" (Neh 9:6).[38] He means that YHWH alone is God, that there is no other God but YHWH. He continues by confessing that YHWH made everything, which includes the heavens and all the angels as well as the earth and the seas and everything in them. This confession allows for no possibility of belief in a rival god.

In response to the idolatry of his time, the prophet Isaiah insists that YHWH, Israel's God, is the only God and that there is no other god besides him in spite of what human beings generally believe. In a trial scene for the purpose of determining who is God, YHWH as the plaintiff calls upon the Israelites as his witnesses to judge in favor of the verdict that he alone is God (even though they are said to be blind and deaf) (Isa 43:8–13; see 43:8, 10a, 12b).[39] The nations are challenged to produce their own witnesses to testify to the reality of their gods, which they fail to do; the implication is that there are no witnesses because the other gods are not the true God (43:9c). Israel can testify to the reality of YHWH in its own history: "It is I who have declared and saved and proclaimed" (43:12a).[40] That YHWH is God is proven by his unprecedented acts and his foretelling of what will happen in human history, which, of course, assumes that YHWH is in control of it.[41] Similarly, defending his claim to exclusive deity against his human detractors, YHWH

---

35. Hobbs, *2 Kings*, 270–71; 277–78.

36. For parallels to God as the living God, see Deut 5:26; Josh 3:10; 1 Sam 17:26, 36; 2 Kgs 19:4; Ps 42:2; 84:2; Isa 37:4, 17; Jer 10:10; 23:36; Dan 6:20, 26; Hos 1:10.

37. אתה יהוה אלהים לבדך. See parallels in 1 Sam 17:45–46 and 1 Kgs 18:37.

38. אתה־הוא יהוה לבדך

39. See Isa 41:1–5; 21–29.

40. אנכי הגדתי והושעתי והשמעתי

41. Hanson, *Isaiah 40–66*, 66–71; Westermann, *Isaiah 40–66*, 119–26; Goldingay, *Message of Isaiah*, 40–55; 197–205.

declares "I am he" and then states in parallelism, "Before me there was no god formed, and after me there will be none" (43:10).⁴² For YHWH to say "I am he" is to say that he alone is God and there is not other God (see Deut 32:39). There has never been nor ever can be a rival god because only YHWH is everlasting: there is no god before YHWH and any god that arises after YHWH could not be a true rival to YHWH since such a being would not be everlasting in nature. The everlasting God stands in contrast to the gods of the nations, who have come into existence in some way, sometimes through sexual procreation as described in the many ancient Near Eastern theogonies. The same thing is meant by the declaration "I, I am YHWH" (43:11).⁴³ Because he is God, there is no savior besides YHWH who can help Israel (43:11b, 12a). The argument for YHWH's uniqueness is based upon his power to deliver, in contrast to any other god that Israel may recognize (see Hos 13:4). Along the same lines, YHWH declares, "From the beginning, I am he" (43:13).⁴⁴ Because he alone is God, no one can thwart YHWH's will: "I act and who can reverse it" (43:13).

In another trial scene (Isa 44:6–23), YHWH proclaims through the prophet Isaiah, "I am the first and I am the last, and there is no God besides me" (44:6).⁴⁵ To be the first and the last is idiomatic of being everlasting and therefore unoriginate; it is also to be transcendent and encompassing of all human history. YHWH alone is God insofar as to be from "the first and the last" is only true of YHWH.⁴⁶ YHWH also states that "there is no god besides me."⁴⁷ The prepositional phrase "besides me" can be interpreted to mean that the gods of the nations do not even exist without YHWH. He then asks rhetorically "Who is like me?" (וּמִי־כָמוֹנִי) (44:7). The expected response is that nothing is comparable to YHWH, since YHWH is nothing like what he transcends. YHWH shows himself to be the only God through the fulfillment of prophecy (44:7–8). He asks, "Have I not long since announced it to you and declared it? And you are my witnesses. Is there any God besides me?" (44:8).⁴⁸

---

42. אני הוא לפני לא־נוצר אל ואחרי לא יהיה
43. אנכי אנכי יהוה
44. גם־מיום אני הוא
45. אני ראשון ואני אחרון ומבלעדי אין אלהים
46. Oswalt, *Isaiah 40–66*, 171.
47. ומבלעדי אין אלהים
48. היש אלוה מבלעדי

The Oneness and Simplicity of God

Through the prophet Isaiah, YHWH reveals to the future Cyrus, identifying him by name (כורש), that he will give to him absolute dominion over the nations (45:1–3) (Cyrus is called by YHWH "my shepherd" in 44:28 and "my anointed" in 45:1). Cyrus is called to his position of absolute rule in order to serve as YHWH's salvation-historical instrument through which he will accomplish his purposes for Israel (45:4). When he ascends to power as foretold, Cyrus then will know that YHWH is the one and only God: "I am YHWH, and there is no other; except me there is no God" (45:5).[49] Joined to the statement "there is no other" in synthetic parallelism is the clause "except me there is no God." The assumption is that only the one true God can act in such a unilateral manner without the possibility of being thwarted or having his purposes compromised. A similar assertion is made in the next verse: "There is no one besides me. I am YHWH, and there is no other" (45:6).[50] Coupled with the statement "I am YHWH, and there is no other" is the synthetically-parallel declaration, "there is no one besides me." This confession will be made not only by Cyrus but by human beings generally in consequence of witnessing YHWH's power in directing human history.[51] In Isa 45:14–17 the prophet predicts that in the future non-Israelites will recognize that Israel's God, YHWH, is the one and only God. They will thereafter abandon idolatry: "Surely, God is with you, and there is no other, not another God" (45:14; see Isa 60:3–14).[52] In apposition to the clause "there is no other" is the phrase "not another God." God is also said to have been hidden (מסתתר), probably because the confession that there is one God is difficult to make given the distorting and desensitizing effect of Israel's long history of involvement with idolatry. Or it could be a confession that the one true God is incomprehensible to human beings, unlike the gods in pagan mythologies (45:15). Likewise, following a description of YHWH as creator of the heavens and the earth, the prophet reports that YHWH declares that there is no other God: "I am YHWH, and there is no other (God)" (Isa 45:18).[53] The implication is that necessarily the creator of all is the one true God. In Isa 45:20–25, YHWH addresses those who have survived the fall of Babylon ("survivors of the nations") through

---

49. אני יהוה ואין עוד זולתי אין אלהים
50. כי־אפס בלעדי אני יהוה ואין עוד
51. Oswalt, *Isaiah 40–66*, 201–3; Smith, *Isaiah 40–66*, 255–57.
52. אך בך אל ואין עוד אפס אלהים
53. אני יהוה ואין עוד. See Goldingay, *Message of Isaiah*, 40–55; 289–90.

the prophet, exhorting them to abandon their ineffectual wooden idols and to come to him as savior (see Isa 44:17–18). He states that he alone is God: "Am I not YHWH? And there is no other God besides me" (Isa 45:21).[54] Because he is the only God, YHWH is the only savior. Warrant for belief that YHWH alone is God and savior is the fact that the fall of Babylon and the rise of Cyrus are foretold before they will occur.[55] The assumption is that only God can know this so long before it happens because God is the one who brings it about.

After exposing the Babylonian gods Bel and Nebo as ineffectual idols (46:5–7), YHWH says through the prophet Isaiah that the Israelites should remember the past deeds that he performed: "Remember the former things long past" (46:9).[56] What YHWH has done will prove that he is the one and only God: "I am God, and there is no other God; I am God, and there is no one like me" (46:9).[57] The statement "there is no other God" is in apposition to the assertion that "there is no one like me." If YHWH alone is God then nothing can be like him.[58] Not only has YHWH performed unequaled deeds to which there is nothing comparable in Babylonian history, but also foretells them before they occur (46:10; see also Isa 41:2–4, 25–26; 42:9; 43:9; 44:7–8; 45:21).[59]

The prophet Jeremiah confesses, "There is none like you, YHWH," by which is meant that there is no God except YHWH; proof of this is YHWH's greatness: "You are great, and great is your name in might" (Jer 10:6).[60] An-

---

54. הלוא אני יהוה ואין־עוד אלהים מבלעדי

55. Westermann, *Isaiah 40–66*, 174–76.

56. Gnostic interpreters subvert the intention of Isa 45:5–6 and 46:9 by claiming that YHWH the creator (demiurge) *wrongly* thought that he was the only God, being ignorant of the true Father, the pleroma and even his mother, Sophia or Achamoth. He did not know his true nature as animal substance and his origin outside the pleroma as a result of the conversion of his mother (see Irenaeus, *Adv. Haer.* 1.5.4; 1.30.6). Or as Irenaeus explains, the Gnostics disparagingly call the demiurge "the fruit of defect, and the offspring of ignorance, and describe him as being ignorant of those things which are above" (*Adv. Haer.* 2.28.4).

57. אנכי אל ואין עוד אלהים ואפס כמוני. See Westermann, *Isaiah 40–66*, 183–86; he writes, "The call to have faith means bringing the nation's experience with God in history to bear upon the present" (185).

58. See Hezekiah's confession: "Now, YHWH our God, deliver us from his hand that all the kingdoms of the earth may know that you alone, YHWH, are God" (Isa 37:20).

59. See Isa 64:4: "For from days of old they have not heard or perceived by ear, nor has the eye seen a God besides you, who acts in behalf of the one who waits for him."

60. מאין כמוך יהוה גדול אתה וגדול שמך בגבורה

other way of expressing that only YHWH is God is to say that YHWH is the true God. In a polemical discourse directed against idolatry, Jeremiah confesses, "But YHWH is the true God" (Jer 10:10a) (see 2 Chr 15:3).[61] To be the true God means to be the only God, as opposed to the many false gods of the nations. This is why it is said that there is none like YHWH: since YHWH is the only God, nothing could be like him. Correlates of being the true God is being the living God and the everlasting king (Jer 10:10b). YHWH as the true God is contrasted with the falseness of idols (שֶׁקֶר) (10:14).

The prophet Joel states that, after the day of YHWH, the judgment of the nation, YHWH will restore national prosperity (Joel 2:18–26). At that time, it will become known to all that YHWH is the one and only God: "Thus you will know that I am in the midst of Israel and that I am YHWH your God, and there is no other" (2:27).[62] The argument is that the events of judgment followed by renewed prosperity will be so unexpected and extraordinary that they will only be explainable as YHWH's intervention into the natural order.[63] No other god can do what YHWH does.

In Ps 18, a royal thanksgiving psalm, the king gives thanks to YHWH for his deliverance (see the parallel in 2 Sam 22). In this context, he asserts that only YHWH is God insofar as only he is a deliverer. He asks rhetorically, "For who is God, besides YHWH? And who is a rock, except our God" (Ps 18:31).[64] Because he has no rival, YHWH is qualified to be a "rock" (see also Deut 32:4, 15, 18, 30, 31; 1 Sam 2:2; Ps 19:14).[65] In Ps 86:10, the psalmist connects the fact that God is great because he does marvelous things with the confession that YHWH alone is God: "For you are great and do wondrous deeds; you alone are God."[66] The implication is that there is a causal connection between these two propositions: YHWH can do marvelous things *because* he is the one true God.

In summary, in different ways in the Hebrew Bible YHWH is asserted to be numerically one. Although their existence is not denied, it is clear that, whatever they are exactly, the other gods are not the same as YHWH,

---

61. יהוה אלהים אמת. See Thompson, *Jeremiah*, 323–32; Bruggemann, *A Commentary on Jeremiah: Exile and Homecoming*, 102–7; Allen, *Jeremiah: A Commentary*, 126–27.

62. ואני יהוה אלהיכם ואין עוד

63. Finley, *Joel, Amos and Obadiah: An Exegetical Commentary*, 63–64.

64. מי אלוה מבלעדי יהוה ומי צור זולתי אלהינו

65. Weiser, *The Psalms: A Commentary*, 194; May, *Psalms*, 93–94.

66. גדול אתה עשׂה נפלאות אתה אלהים לבדך. See Tate, *Psalms 51–100*, 381–82.

God as Numerically One

Israel's God, proof of which is YHWH's incomparable acts, including controlling the unfolding of history and foretelling future events.[67] The formula "there is no other" (אֵין עוֹד) is used frequently in order to express YHWH's uniqueness: YHWH is God and *there is no other* (God) (Deut 4:39; Isa 45:5, 6; 45:14, 18; 1 Kgs 8:59–60; Joel 2:27). A variation of this formula is "there is no other God" (אֵין עוֹד אֱלֹהִים) (Isa 45:21; 46:9). The phrase "there is no other" is qualified by a propositional phrase: "there is no other apart from him" (אֵין עוֹד מִלְבַדּוֹ) (Deut 4:35) and "there is no other God besides me" (וְאֵין־עוֹד אֱלֹהִים מִבַּלְעָדַי) (Isa 45:21; see 43:11 [savior]). It is also said that there is no God "besides" (מִבַּלְעָד) (Isa 44:6, 8; Ps 18:31), "except" (זוּלָה) (Isa 45:5; 2 Sam 7:22; Ps 18:31) or "with" (עִמָּד) (Deut 32:39) YHWH. The same thing is intended by saying that there is no one like YHWH (כְּמוֹ) (Exod 15:11; Isa 44:7; 46:9; Jer 10:6, 8). It is also affirmed that "there is no God in all the earth but in Israel (כִּי אִם־בְּיִשְׂרָאֵל)" (2 Kgs 5:15). Likewise, YHWH's uniqueness is expressed by saying that there is not another God (אֶפֶס אֱלֹהִים) (Isa 45:14) and there is "no one besides" him (אֶפֶס בִּלְעָד) (Isa 45:6). Sometimes it is asserted that YHWH is God alone (לְבַד) (2 Kgs 19:15, 19; Neh 9:6; Ps 86:10), that YHWH is the true God (אֱלֹהִים אֱמֶת) (Jer 10) or the living God (אֱלֹהִים חַי) (2 Kgs 19:16). YHWH declares his uniqueness with the statement "I am he" (אֲנִי הוּא) (Deut 32:39; Isa 43:10, 13) and "I, I am YHWH" (אָנֹכִי יְהוָה) (Isa 43:11). Another means of expressing that only YHWH is God is the statement that YHWH is first and last (Isa 44:6) and that before and after YHWH there is no god (Isa 43:10).

God as One in the New Testament

In the New Testament, the monotheism of the Hebrew Bible is assumed: that God is numerically one is foundational. The earliest church inherits the belief in the one God and the repudiation of idolatry that characterizes Second Temple Judaism.[68] Jesus quotes the Shema as the first greatest commandment (see Mark 12:29–30, 32–33), and he speaks about "the one and only God" (τοῦ μόνου θεοῦ) (John 5:44) and the "one and only true God"

---

67. See Exod 12:12; 21:19; Num 33:4; Ruth 2:12.

68. See Pr. Azar. 22; *Sib. Or.* 3.11–12, 545–61; see 4.24–30; 5.172–76, 493–500; *Ep. Arist.* 132–38; Wis. Sol. 13–15; Philo, *Dec.* 52–81; *Mos.* 1.75; *Spec.* 1.1–52; *Leg.* 3.97–99; Josephus, *Ant.* 2.275–76; *Apion* 2.190–98.

(τὸν μόνον ἀληθινὸν θεόν) (John 17:3).[69] According to Jesus, only the one God can be called good, presumably because only the transcendent source of all blessings to human beings can be called *truly* good (Mark 10:17–18). The earliest Jewish followers of the Way confess that YHWH, the God who has been at work in Israel's history, is also the one who sent Jesus, the Righteous One (Acts 7:52). Similarly, James points out that God is one (εἷς ἐστιν ὁ θεός) and that even the demons are compelled to confess this as true (2:19).[70] Finally, in his concluding doxology Jude refers to God as "the only God" (μόνῳ θεῷ),[71] who is further identified as "our savior" (25).[72]

The apostle Paul assumes that the God who in the Hebrew Bible accomplished his salvation-historical purposes in relation to Israel is the same God who raised Jesus from the dead (Acts 13:17–37). In Gal 3:20 he confesses that "God is one,"[73] and in Rom 3:28–30, he argues against Jewish particularism on the basis that there is one God: since God is one, God must be God of both Jews and gentiles (Rom 3:29).[74] For this reason, he confesses God as "one God and Father of all" (Eph 4:6),[75] and in his doxology in 1 Tim 1:17 he refers to God as the "only God" (μόνῳ θεῷ), clearly indicating God's uniqueness (see "only ruler" in 1 Tim 6:15).[76] Paul likewise addresses his doxology at the end of his Letter to

69. The use of the adjective μόνος to signify that God alone is God occurs in Pr. Azar. 22; 2 Macc 1:24–25; 7:37; 4 Macc 5:24; LXX 4 Kgds 19:15, 19; 1 Esdr 8:25; 2 Esdr 19:6 (Neh 9:6); 82:19; 85:10; Dan 3:45. In 2 Kgs 19:15, 19; Neh 9:6 (2 Esdr. 19:6); Ps 82:19, the Hebrew original translated by μόνος is לְבַדְּךָ (see 4Q504 frags. 1–2. col. 5.8–9).

70. Davids, *Commentary on James*, 125–26; Richardson, *James*, 133–35; Moo, *James*, 106–7.

71. In Rev 15:4 God is said to be alone holy (μόνος ὅσιος), which is to say that God is alone God since to be holy is to be divine.

72. Green, *Jude and 2 Peter*, 134.

73. ὁ δὲ θεὸς εἷς ἐστιν. See Fung, *The Epistle to the Galatians*, 158–66; Longenecker, *Galatians*, 139–43. Paul contrasts the plurality involved in the giving of the Law with the one God involved in the giving of the promise to Abraham. The assumption is that what is mediated is inferior to what is non-mediated. He says that the mediator is not one, which seems to mean that a mediator implies two parties, in this case the angels who gave the Law and the Israelites to whom the Law was given. By contrast God is said to be one, which in this context implies the unconditionalty of the promise.

74. The confession that God is one occurs in Hellenistic Judaism (Josephus, *Ant*. 3.91; 4.201; 5.112; *Ep. Arist*. 132; *Sib. Or*. 3.629; Philo, *Opif*. 171).

75. εἷς θεὸς καὶ πατὴρ πάντων. See Lincoln, *Ephesians*, 237–38; O'Brien, *Ephesians*, 284–86.

76. Delling, "ΜΟΝΟΣ ΘΕΟΣ."

the Romans to "the only wise God,"⁷⁷ one possible translation of which is "to the only *and* wise God" (Rom 16:27).⁷⁸ By the term "only" (μόνος) he intends to express God's uniqueness. Similarly, in 1 Tim 2:5 he states that "there is one God" (εἷς θεός).⁷⁹ In dealing with the problems that some of his Corinthian converts are having with eating meat sacrificed to idols, Paul states, "We know that there is no such thing as an idol in the world, and that there is no God but one" (1 Cor 8:4).⁸⁰ He both affirms the existence of one God and denies the existence of other gods besides this one God. Reminiscent of the Shema, Paul adds that there is "but one God the Father (εἷς θεὸς ὁ πατήρ), from whom are all things" (1 Cor 8:6).⁸¹ God is called Father because he is the source or progenitor of all things. To the semantic field of "one God" and "only God" belongs the phrase "true God." Paul calls God "the living and true God" (θεῷ ζῶντι καὶ ἀληθινῷ) in 1 Thess 1:9 to distinguish him from the false gods that his Thessalonian converts abandoned when they became believers.⁸² By the term "true God" Paul means that there is only one real God; whatever the other so-called gods are they are not the same as God.⁸³

In continuity with Second Temple Jewish sources, it becomes unambiguously clear in the New Testament that pagan gods are actually demons and therefore not unreal, fictitious beings.⁸⁴ This comes to expression in

77. μόνῳ σοφῷ θεῷ

78. Dupont, "ΜΟΝΩΙ ΣΟΦΩΙ ΘΕΩΙ (Rom 16:27)"; Dunn, *Romans 9–16*, 916.

79. Marshall, *The Pastoral Epistles*, 404–6.

80. οὐδεὶς θεὸς εἰ μὴ εἷς.

81. Fee, *The First Epistle to the Corinthians*, 373–78; Horsley, *1 Corinthians*, 119–20; Garland, *1 Corinthians*, 373–74.

82. θεῷ ζῶντι καὶ ἀληθινῷ. See Witherington, *1 and 2 Thessalonians: A Socio-Rhetorical Commentary*, 73–74.

83. The phrase "true God" occurs in polemical contexts in the Hebrew Bible and 3 Maccabees, where false, idolatrous gods are set in contrast to God: אֱלֹהֵי אֱמֶת in 2 Chr 15:3; אֱלֹהִים אֱמֶת in Jer 10:10; ἀληθινὸς θεός in 3 Macc 6:18; see 2:11.

84. According to *1 Enoch* and the *Book of Jubilees*, the Watchers morally corrupted human beings by teaching them to do evil (*1 En.* 7–8, 69; 10; 21:7–10; 64–65; 69; *Jub.* 5:1, 6–11; 8:3). In *1 Enoch* 19, it is explained that after the flood, the bodies of the angels are imprisoned, whereas their spirits are free to roam the earth until the final judgment. These spirits lead human beings astray; in particular, they entice them to offer sacrifices to demons (*daimonia*) as unto gods. It is possible that the term "demons" refers not to the Watchers but to their disembodied offspring. If so, then *1 En.* 19 is made consistent with *1 En.* 15:8–12. According to the *Book of Jubilees*, with the assistance of subordinate spirits, Mastema encourages human beings to become idolators: "And they began making graven images and polluted likenesses. And cruel spirits assisted them and led them

The Oneness and Simplicity of God

Paul's explanation to the Corinthians concerning what they should do about visiting pagan temples. Paul instructs them to shun idolatry (1 Cor 10:14).[85] In particular, he tells them to avoid pagan temples because to eat a meal there is to have communion with demons. This is because the sacrifices offered in pagan temples are offered to demons and not to God (1 Cor 10:20).

Confession of One God by the Early Church

The writings of the Apostolic Fathers testify to the early church's conviction that God is numerically one.[86] According to *Shepherd of Hermas* the first commandment is to believe that God is one and the creator of all things: "First of all believe that God is one, who made all things and perfected them, and made all things to be from that which is not" (*Man.* 1.1; see *Vis.* 1.3.4).[87] In order to distinguish God from all created things and express his uniqueness, it is further explained that God contains all things (πάντα χωρῶν) and is contained by nothing (ἀχώρητος) (1.1). The assumption is that there can be only one "container" of all things. Clement of Rome refers to God as creator (δημιουργός) and ruler of all (*1 Clem.* 8.2; 20.11; 33.2) as well as the synonymous title "Father and creator of everything" (19.2).[88] The implication of these designations is that there is only one God. He also refers to God as "the only invisible God" (*2 Clem.* 20.5).[89] The same confession of one creator and ruler of all things is found in *Epistle of Barnabas* (19.2; 21.5) and the *Didache* (1.2; 10.3).[90]

Because of their rejection of the pagan gods and their belief in the absurdity of idolatry, early Christians had to defend themselves against the charge of being atheists.[91] Given the antiquity of belief in them, it was held to be undeniable that the Greek and Roman gods existed—an *argumentum ad*

---

astray so that they might commit sin and pollution. And the prince Mastema acted forcefully to do all this" (*Jub.* 11:4). Likewise, in the Letter of Enoch, idolatry is identified as worshipping demons (*1 En.* 99:7), and in *1 Bar.* 4:7 the people are chastised for sacrificing to demons and not God.

85. Fee, *The First Epistle to the Corinthians*, 462–65; Harrington, *1 Corinthians*, 375–82.

86. Kelly, *Early Christian Doctrines*, 83.

87. εἷς ἐστιν ὁ θεός.

88. δεσπότης τῶν ἁπάντων / ὁ πατὴρ καὶ κτιστὴς τοῦ σύμπαντος.

89. τῷ μόνῳ θεῷ ἀοράτῳ.

90. From a slightly later period, see Origen, *Prin.* 1, praef. 4; Novatian, *De Trin.* 4, 31.

91. See Eusebius, *Praep. ev.* 1.2.1–5; Athenagoras, *Leg.* 1–7 (3–7).

populum. Not to acknowledge and worship them could only mean atheism, since there was no other religious option. Justin writes, "And we confess that we are atheists, so far as gods of this sort are concerned, but not with respect to the most true God" (*1 Apol*. 6).[92] In continuity with Hellenistic Judaism, the Apologists, those early church fathers who undertook to defend Christianity against attack from paganism, confess their belief in the one true God and delineate how he differs from the Greek and Roman gods. They also seek to explain the true nature of the gods and how belief in them arose.[93] These views are reiterated by subsequent Christian theologians.

The true God is distinguished from the Greek and Roman gods. The use of a common name (θεός or *deus*) for both God and the gods conceals the absolute difference between them. For this reason, Tertullian considers it inappropriate that the one true God should share a name in common with the gods because they have nothing in common by which to justify sharing a name. He points out that the one true God is not a possible sensible object, unlike the gods: "But the true God, on the sole ground that he is not an object of sense, is incapable of being compared with those false deities which are cognizable to sight and sense" (*Ad nat*. 2.4.6–8).[94] In addition, different from the gods, who are believed to have come into existence, the one true God is said to be ingenerate and therefore eternal. Theophilus of Antioch explains, "And he is without beginning, because he is ingenerate" (*Ad Autol*. 1.4).[95] There is an absolute difference between the divine and the non-divine, as Athenagoras states: "For, a thing is either ingenerate and eternal or generate and perishable" (*Leg*. 19).[96] He argues that insofar as they are sensibly depictable as idols the Greek gods cannot be true gods.[97] This is because whatever is perceived by the senses is composed of matter and things composed of matter are created with the result that they also are dissoluble and perishable

---

92. Barnard, *Justin Martyr: His Life and Thought*, 75–84; Osborn, *Justin Martyr*, 17–27, 55–64.

93. Although in some cases arguments are presented to defend monotheism, in general the apologists polemicize on the assumption that belief in one God is something that all human beings already acknowledge in some way. Sometimes they make use of Greek philosophical conceptual categories in their disputation with their religious background.

94. Porro θεός ille iam hoc solo quod non sit in promptu, vacat a comparatione eorum qui in promptu sunt et visui et sensui. See Dunn, *Tertullian*.

95. ἄναρχος δέ ἐστιν, ὅτι ἀγέννητός ἐστιν (see 2.36). See Rogers, *Theophilus of Antioch: The Life and Thought of a Second-Century Bishop*, part 2.

96. ἢ γὰρ ἀγένητόν τι καὶ ἔστιν ἀΐδιον, ἢ γεννητόν καὶ φθαρτόν ἐστι.

97. Rankin, *Athenagoras. Philosopher and Theologian*, 73–128.

The Oneness and Simplicity of God

(τὰ λυτὰ καὶ φθαρτὰ) (*Leg.* 15). By contrast, God is by definition ingenerate (ἀγένητος) and eternal (ἀΐδιος) (*Leg.* 15).[98] Justin refers to God "the *only* ingenerate God" (θεῷ δὲ μόνῳ τῷ ἀγεννήτῳ) (*1 Apol.* 14), because the one true God alone is characterized by ingenerateness.[99] Similarly, Tertullian claims that by definition God has eternity, which means having neither a beginning nor an end (*Ad nat.* 2.3.5).[100]

As ingenerate and eternal, God is the creator of all things. After rejecting as hopelessly inconsistent the accounts of the gods put forward by philosophers, Theophilus of Antioch writes, "Now we also confess that God exists, but that he is one, the creator, and maker, and fashioner of this universe; and we know that all things are arranged by his providence, but by him alone" (*Ad Autol.* 3.9).[101] Similarly, Tatian expresses God's uniqueness as creator by saying that God is the substance of all things, visible and invisible[102] and all power[103] (*Or.* 5).[104] Under the influence of Platonism, Justin asserts that the ingenerate (ἀγέν[υ]ητος) God is the cause of all that is generate (τὸ γινόμενον) (*1 Apol.* 14, 25, 49, 53; *2 Apol.* 6, 12, 13; *Dial.* 5, 94, 114, 126, 127). Often the Platonic term "Father" is used of God as creator and progenitor of all things.[105] Alluding to Plato's statement in the *Timaeus*,

---

98. τὸ μὲν γὰρ θεῖον ἀγένητον εἶναι καὶ ἀΐδιον . . . καὶ δὲ ὕλην γενητὴν καὶ φθαρτήν. For God as unbegotten see 4, 6, 8, 10, 22, 23, 30 and as eternal see 4, 6, 10, 15, 21, 23, 26, 30.

99. See also "to the good and unbegotten God" (ἀγαθῷ καὶ ἀγεννήτῳ θεῷ) (*1 Apol.* 14); "unbegotten and impassible" (ἀγενήτῳ καὶ ἀπαθεῖ) (*1 Apol.* 25); "to the unbegotten God" (τῷ ἀγεννήτῳ θεῷ) (*1 Apol.* 49); "to the unbegotten God" (τῷ ἀγεννήτῳ θεῷ) (*1 Apol.* 53); and "the Father of everything and unbegotten God" (τὸν πατέρα τῶν ὅλων καὶ ἀγέννητον θεὸν) (*Dial.* 114).

100. "That essential character of divinity, eternity, which is reckoned to be without beginning, and without end" (substantia divinitatis, id est aeternitate, quae sine initio et fine censetur).

101. ἡμεῖς δὲ καὶ θεὸν ὁμολογοῦμεν, ἀλλ' ἕνα, τὸν κτίστην καὶ ποιητὴν καὶ δημιουργὸν τοῦδε τοῦ παντός, καὶ προνοίᾳ τὰ πάντα διοικεῖσθαι ἐπιστάμεθα, ἀλλ' ὑπ' αὐτοῦ μόνου. Theophilus writes that God "alone is the source and fountain of all good (bonorum omnium solus caput et fons), the creator, founder, and framer of all that endures, by whom all things on earth and all in heaven are quickened, and filled with the stir of life, and without whom there would assuredly be nothing to bear any name, and have any substance?" (*Ad Autol.* 2.2).

102. αὐτὸς ὑπάρχων τοῦ παντὸς ἡ ὑπόστασις / ὁρατῶν τε καὶ ἀοράτων αὐτὸς ὑπόστασις.

103. πᾶσα δύναμις.

104. Hunt, *Christianity in the 2nd Century: The Case of Tatian*.

105. Justin, *1 Apol.* 6, 8, 12, 32, 40, 44, 45, 46, 61; *2 Apol.* 6; *Dial.* 7, 32, 56, 58, 60, 61,

Justin refers to God as "Father and creator of all things," who stands in opposition to the many gods of Homer and other poets (*2 Apol.* 10).[106] According to Arnobius, the difference between God and the gods is absolute insofar as God as ingenerate and immortal created all things, including the gods (*Adv. nat.* 1.28, 30, 32; 2.2, 35, 36, 44, 45, 72; 3.3, 4, 5).[107]

The Apologists are unanimous that the many gods of the Greeks and Romans are actually demons who masquerade as gods, leading human beings away from the one true God. These created spirits attach themselves to images of the dead, which is the origin of idolatry. Justin interprets LXX Ps 96:5 (95:5) "the gods of the nations are *daimonia*"[108] to mean that the gods of the gentiles are not fictional beings but actually demonic entities (*Dial.* 55; 73; 79; 83; 91). Alluding to the account of the Watchers found in the Book of Watchers in *1 Enoch* and other sources, he explains that human beings misidentify the angels and their demon offspring as gods (*2 Apol.* 5). Similarly, drawing upon *1 Enoch*, Tertullian asserts that demons, the offspring of the Watchers, incite human beings to idolatry (*De idol.* 4).[109] He quotes from the Letter of Enoch to the effect that idolators are actually worshipping demons (*1 En.* 99:7). Minucius Felix has Octavius propose a twofold explanation of the origin of belief in the traditional Greek and Roman gods. First, he says that it is the result of the euhemeristic deification of human beings who lived in the distant past (*Oct.* 20–23). He explains, however, that human beings cannot actually become gods because what is divine by definition is neither born nor dies: "But that is divine which has neither rising nor setting" (*Oct.* 23).[110] Second, Octavius asserts that behind the traditional gods lurk demons who exploit the fact that human beings mistakenly deify people of the past (*Oct.* 26–27). This explains supernatural activities associated with the gods and their idols. In addition, the deification of the material elements is rejected as mistaken because whatever is material cannot by definition be God.[111] Theophilus of Antioch explains

---

63, 74, 75, 76, 105, 108, 114, 115, 127, 128, 133, 140; Athenagoras, *Leg.* 6, 10, 16, 24, 27; Theophilus of Antioch, *Ad Autol.* 1.4; 2.13.

106. τὸν δὲ πατέρα καὶ δημιουργὸν πάντων.

107. McCracken, *Arnobius of Sicca: The Case against the Pagans: Books 1–3*.

108. ὅτι πάντες οἱ θεοὶ τῶν ἐθνῶν δαιμόνια ὁ δὲ κύριος τοὺς οὐρανοὺς ἐποίησεν.

109. Waszink and Van Winden, *Tertullianus De Idolatria. Critical Text and Commentary*, 100–122; Binder, *Tertullian, On Idolatry and Mishnah Abodah Zarah*, 61–82.

110. Divinum autem id est quod nec ortum habet nec occasum.

111. See Aristides, *Apologia* 3–5; Melito of Sardis.

that by positing the eternity of matter, "God is no longer . . . creator of all things, nor is the monarchy of God established" (*Ad Autol.* 2.4; see 2.13).[112]

Some early Christian theologians go beyond Scripture and affirm that God cannot but be one. In other words, they hold that God is not only numerically one but is *necessarily* so. Based on a geo-centric cosmology, Athengoras argues that there cannot be another God since there would no place (τόπος) where that God could be (*Leg.* 8). God completely occupies the spatial realm beyond the outermost heavenly sphere, which is referred to as "around the world" (περὶ τὸν κόσμον). In addition, Athengoras assumes that another God could not be somewhere in the world (ἐν τῷ κόσμῳ), as opposed to around the world, because such a God would have no right to be in a world that he did not create and does not govern (*Leg.* 8). Similarly, Lactantius seeks to undermine polytheism by demonstrating that from a correct understanding of the divine nature it follows that God is necessarily one (D.I. 1.3). According to him, the reason that many gods are required for the governance of the world can only be that none is capable of doing it on its own. When being perfect is defined as being that "to which nothing can be added," it follows that none of the traditional Greek and Roman gods is perfect, since to each can add greater power. Lactantius takes it as axiomatic, however, that God by definition has the property of perfection, from which it follows that God can only be one since being perfect requires having all possible power ("in whom the whole is") and therefore having no need of assistance in the governance of the world. He writes, "But God, if he is perfect, as he ought to be, cannot but be one, because he is perfect, so that all things may be in him."[113] By the statement that all things are "in" God, he probably means that all things are subordinate to God. Along the same lines, adopting the conceptual framework of middle Platonism, Clement of Alexandria identifies the biblical God with the Platonic first principle (ἀρχή).[114] He connects Deut 6:4 "the Lord your God is one" with the statement made by Timaeus the Locrian, known from Plato's *Timaeus*, that there is "one first principle of all things" (μία

---

112. οὐκ ἔτι ὁ θεὸς ποιητὴς τῶν ὅλων ἐστὶ . . . οὐδὲ μὴν μοναρχία θεοῦ δείκνυται.

113. Deus vero perfectus est (quia perfectus est) ut esse debet, non potest esse nisi unus, ut in eo sint Omnia.

114. Other references to God as first include: *Strom.* 4.25 "first principle of action" (ἀρχῆς ποιητικός); 5.6 "the first principle of everything" (ἡ τῶν ὅλων ἀρχή); 5.12 "the first principle of all things" (ἀρχὴ παντός); and 7.17 "an imitation of the one first principle" (μίμημα ὂν ἀρχῆς τῆς μιᾶς).

ἀρχὰ πάτων) (*Strom.* 5.14). The one God of the Hebrew Scriptures thereby becomes the necessarily-one God and first principle of middle Platonism.

The fact that God is necessarily one becomes part of the early church's strategy in refuting Marcionism.[115] Tertullian argues against Marcion and others who postulate a second God, who is the creator and identified with YHWH of the Hebrew Bible, that "God is not, if he is not one" (Deus si non unus est, non est) (*Adv. Marc.* 1.3).[116] The argument that he offers in

---

115. In both heretical systems, the depiction of YHWH in the Hebrew Bible is thought to be unworthy of the true God. In addition, the creation of the material world is viewed as a mistake, and so cannot be attributed to the true God, who would not do something so foolish and base. The only conclusion that can be reached is that a lesser divine being is responsible for it, the God of the Hebrew Bible.

116. See Osborn, *Tertullian: First Theologian of the West*, chap. 5. Known primarily through the writings of Justin, Tertullian, and Irenaeus, Marcion introduces the heresy that the God of the Hebrew Bible is a different God from the God revealed by Jesus Christ, who was unknown to human beings before that time. According to Irenaeus, Polycarp refuses to acknowledge Marcion as a legitimate teacher: "And Polycarp himself replied to Marcion, who met him on one occasion, and said, 'Do you know me?' 'I do know you, the first-born of Satan'" (*Adv. Haer.* 3.3.4). In a work called *Antitheses*, Marcion contrasts sayings of and statements about YHWH with Jesus' teachings about the God whom he represents. A fundamental difference between the two Gods is that YHWH is characterized as just, whereas Jesus' God is good. According to Tertullian, Marcion applies Luke 6:43 "For there is no good tree which produces bad fruit, nor, on the other hand, a bad tree which produces good fruit," to the latter, and concludes that this God, being good, can do nothing to cause suffering, even if such an act is retributive justice (*Adv. Marc.* 1.2; 2.14). For Marcion being good precludes being just, because being just requires judging, which in turn involves inflicting punishment, a form of evil (*Adv. Marc.* 2.11; 5.4–5; Irenaeus, *Adv. Haer.* 3.25.3; 4.28.1). In antithesis to this characterization of the good God, Marcion finds statements from YHWH in the Hebrew Bible, such Isa 45:7 "I . . . create evil" (ἐγὼ . . . κτίζων κακά) and Jer 18:11 "I am preparing evil for you" (ἐγὼ πλάσσω ἐφ' ὑμᾶς κακά). He concludes that such statements could not be made by the good God, on the assumption that the attributes of goodness and justice are incompatible. To bring evil (κακά) upon another as an act of retributive justice is impossible for a good God, but not for a just God. The only possible conclusion is that there are two Gods, a just God, YHWH, and a good God, whom, Marcion claims, is unknown to the just God, who thinks that he is the only God, which explains the many statements in the Hebrew Bible that YHWH alone is God (*Adv. Marc.* 1.11). The Mosaic Law belongs to the just God, whereas the gospel belongs to the good God. Jesus Christ, known from a mutilated version of Luke's Gospel, is from the good God, hithero unknown, and is not the Messiah foretold in the Hebrew Bible, who will be sent later by the just God.

It would seem that Marcion claims that the two Gods are equal, and therefore are two originative principles. Tertullian explains, "The heretic of Pontus introduces two Gods . . . one whom it was impossible to deny, i.e., our creator; and one whom he will never be able to prove, i.e., his own God" (*Adv. Marc.* 1.2). According to Irenaeus, Marcion's two Gods differ from each only in that one is good and the other evil: "There are two beings,

The Oneness and Simplicity of God

support of this view depends on the universally accepted definition of God as "the great supreme existing in eternity, unbegotten, unmade without beginning, without end."[117] If God is the great supreme, then nothing can be equal to God. Only the unique (*unicum*), however, can have no equal, from which it follows that God cannot be other than one. As Tertullian expresses it, "Surely it must be that nothing is equal to him, i.e., that there is no other great supreme; because, if there were, he would have an equal; and if he had an equal, he would be no longer the great supreme." For this reason, the existence of Marcion's two Gods is a logical impossibility.

Gods by nature, differing from each other, the one being good (*bonum*), but the other evil (*malum*)" (*Adv. Haer.* 3.12.12). Hippolytus even describes the two Gods as equal, co-eternal principles: "Marcion . . . supposed (the existence of) two originating causes of the universe, alleging one of them to be a certain good (principle), but the other an evil one" (7.17). Nevertheless, in spite of the fact that he claims that the two Gods are equal, Marcion clearly has a preference for the good God over the just God, which calls into question their true equality. As Tertullian explains, "For the rest, however, we know full well that Marcion makes his Gods unequal: one judicial, harsh, mighty in war; the other mild, placid, and simply good and excellent" (*Adv. Marc.* 1.6). So it is unclear how for Marcion these two Gods relate to each other ontologically. It is probable, however, that he subordinates the just God to the good God, which explains Irenaeus' statement that Marcion "holds that there are two Gods, separated from each other by an infinite distance (*infinita distantia separatos ab invicem*)" (*Adv. Haer.* 4.33.2). What he means by this is not clear but this description may imply the ontological supremacy of the good God. This hypothesis also makes sense of Justin's statement that Marcion taught his followers "to deny that God is the maker of this universe, and to assert that some other being, greater than he, has done greater works" (*1 Apol* 26; see 58). Greater works are performed by the greater God. The just God created the universe from pre-existing matter and for that reason is called the kosmocrator (*Adv. Marc.* 1.15; Irenaeus, *Adv. Haer.* 3.11.12). The implication, however, is that creating a material universe is an act unworthy of the supreme God, especially since matter is the principle of evil.

It is not surprising to find Marcion criticizing YHWH, the just God, for being inconsistent and actually unjust at times. Marcion cites several examples of such questionable behavior. Irenaeus writes about Marcion: "He advanced the most daring blasphemy against him who is proclaimed as God by the law and the prophets, declaring him to be the author of evils, to take delight in war, to be infirm of purpose, and even to be contrary to himself" (*Adv. Haer.* 1.27.2). The fact that YHWH removed the kingship from Saul and gave it to David, much to Samuel's distress (1 Sam 15:11), is cited as an example of his arbitrariness (Tertullian, *Adv. Marc.* 2.23–24). Other objectionable actions of YHWH, the so-called just God, include his hardening of Pharaoh's heart (Irenaeus, *Adv. Haer.* 4.29.1; Tertullian, *Adv. Marc.* 2.24) and his commandment to the Israelites to despoil their Egyptian neighbors before leaving Egypt (Irenaeus, *Adv. Haer.* 4.30.1; Tertullian, *Adv. Marc.* 2.20; 4.24; 5.13). Such things are morally questionable, according to Marcion, unworthy of a legitimate God.

117. Deum summum esse magnum, in aeternitate constitutum, innatum, infectum, sine initio, sine fine. See Tertullian *De virg. vel.* 1.

2

From God as Numerically One to God as Simple

CHRISTIAN THEOLOGIANS HOLD TO the biblical view that God is numerically one, and they further conclude that God is necessarily so. In addition, however, they have affirmed that there is another, more fundamental type of oneness attributable to God. God is one not merely in the sense of being the only God, but also in the sense of being simple or non-composite, having no parts of any kind. A created thing is a unity because it is one thing; nevertheless, in spite of being one thing, it is not an absolute unity since it is composed of different types of parts. By contrast, God is said to be an absolute unity. With a few exceptions, the simplicity doctrine was maintained for centuries by Christian theologians without any hint that it is mistaken or meaningless.

Origin in Greek Philosophy

The idea that God is simple enters Christian theology through the influence of Greek philosophy, either directly or as mediated by Hellenistic Judaism. Plato holds that God is simple (ἁπλοῦς) and unchanging (*Rep.* 380d–383c). He writes, "Then God is altogether simple (κομιδῇ ἄρα ὁ θεὸς ἁπλοῦν) and true in deed and word, and neither changes himself nor deceives others by visions or words or the sending of signs" (382e).[1] For Plato there is a correlation between being unchanging and being simple, since change requires having parts, physical or non-physical. Implicitly it

---

1. See *Tim.* 41a–b.

is considered an ontological value to be as unchanging as possible, on the assumption that what is perfect does not change in any respect, since any change would be towards the imperfect. It follows that, since it is incapable of change, a simple thing has greater value than a composite thing. In addition, in the dialogue *Parmenides*, it is explained that Parmenides's One, which arguably should be considered divine in a pantheistic sense, can have no parts (μέρη).[2] It cannot even be a whole (ὅλον) since a whole is that from which no part is lacking. Because of this, the One is unlimited insofar as it has no beginning or end, is formless, is not in place, and is neither in motion (by changing into something else or by moving in place) nor is at rest (*Parm.* 137c–139b; see 142c–d [μέρη]; 159c [μόρια]).[3] It likewise follows that no predicate is attributable to the One, not even oneness or being (τό τε ἕν καὶ τὸ ὄν) (142c–143b). In other words, it cannot be said that the One is *one* or that the One *is*, because this presupposes that the One has parts: oneness and being.[4] It is clear that Plato is sympathetic to aspects of Parmenides's philosophical monism.

Like Plato, Aristotle associates being simple with being unchangeable.[5] In his theological reflections, he observes that the first motion caused by the unmoved mover, the rotation of the first heavenly sphere, is one and simple since it is in continuous, circular motion. Arguing from effect to cause, he concludes that the unmoved mover must likewise be simple and unchanging. He writes, "But the unmoved mover ... since it remains permanently simple (ἁπλῶς) and unvarying and in the same state, will cause motion that is one and simple" (μίαν καὶ ἁπλῆν) (*Phys.* 8.6; 260a 16–18). He does not elaborate on what it means for the unmoved mover to be simple in this context, but by analogy with the simple motion of the first heavenly sphere, the unmoved mover no doubt is uniformly one. He further concludes that the first mover is indivisible and without parts (ἀδιαίρετον ... καὶ ἀμερές), in addition to being without magnitude (*Phys.* 8.10; 267b 25–26). In *Metaphysics*, Aristotle asserts that what is first is primary being (ἡ οὐσία πρώτη), by which he means substance (τὸ ὑποκείμενον), "that of which everything else is predicated, while it is itself not predicated of anything else" (*Metaph.* 7.3; 1028b 36–37). What is first among primary beings is the primary being that is a simple, fully-actual

---

2. Dodds, "The Parmenides of Plato and the Origin of the Neoplatonic 'One.'"
3. See also the discussion in *Soph.* 245a–c.
4. Dancy, *Two Studies in the Early Academy*, 96–98.
5. Stead, *Divine Substance*, 89–109.

substance (καὶ ταύτης ἡ ἁπλῆ καὶ κατ' ἐνέργειαν), which is to say, the first mover that eternally causes the first heavenly sphere to rotate (*Metaph.* 12.7; 1072a32–33). Aristotle refers to God the first mover as "without parts and indivisible" (ἀμερὴς καὶ ἀδιαίρετός ἐστιν) (*Metaph.* 12.7; 1073a 7).[6] He is committed to the view that God is a substance in the sense of a being, for otherwise God could not be the first mover. As a substance, however, God is unique insofar as he is simple or without parts, among other unique attributes, such as being eternal, necessary, unmoved and unmovable, fully actual and devoid of potentiality.

Middle Platonic philosophers are more explicit that God, identical to Plato's One and Good, is one in the sense of being simple or incomposite.[7] Again a correlation is assumed to exist between being unchanging and being simple: what is simple by definition cannot change since change requires having parts.[8] On the assumption that Ammonius's speech about the meaning of the letter E at the temple of Apollo reflects Plutarch's own views, it is clear that Plutarch holds that there is one God devoid of all plurality (*De E* 393a–c).[9] He identifies God with the One,[10] by which is probably meant the Platonic One; the One is said to be eternally the same, timeless and unmoving (*De E* 393a).[11] He refers to the One as "that which

---

6. Aristotle asserts that the necessary is the simple (*Metaph.* 5.5; 1015b11–12).

7. Zeller, *Grundriss der Geschichte der Griechischen Philosophie*, 283–310; Grant, *Gods and the One God*, 75–83; Dillon, *The Middle Platonists*; Carabine, *The Unknown God*, 51–102; Hägg, *Clement of Alexandria and the Beginnings of Christian Apophaticism*, 72–133.

8. Antiochus of Aschalon is said to hold that the Ideas are "always simple and of one kind" (semper esset simplex et unius modi), unlike sensible things (Cicero, *Acad.* VIII. 30); the Ideas exist as thoughts in the mind of the creating God (Seneca, *Epist.* 65, 7) (Osborn, *The Philosophy of Clement of Alexandria*, 19).

9. Dillon, *The Middle Platonists*, 184–230 (190–91). John Whittaker identifies a neo-Pythagorean influence on Ammonius's view ("Ammonius on the Dephic E"; "Philological Comments on the Neoplatonic Notion of Infinity").

10. ἀλλ' ἔστιν ὁ θεός, χρὴ φάναι, καὶ ἔστι κατ' οὐδένα χρόνον ἀλλὰ κατὰ τὸν αἰῶνα τὸν ἀκίνητον καὶ ἄχρονον καὶ ἀνέγκλιτον καὶ οὗ πρότερον οὐδέν ἐστιν οὐδ' ὕστερον οὐδὲ μέλλον οὐδὲ παρῳχημένον οὐδὲ πρεσβύτερον οὐδὲ νεώτερον ἀλλ' εἷς ὢν ἑνὶ τῷ νῦν τὸ ἀεὶ πεπλήρωκε, καὶ μόνον ἐστὶ.

11. Plato is supposed to have delivered a lecture called "On the Good" in which he made the statement "Good is one" (ἀγαθόν ἐστιν ἕν) (Aristoxenus, *Elements of Harmony*). In discussing Plato's doctrine of the Good, Aristotle reveals that Plato and his school hold that the Good is also the One: "On the assumption that goodness is a property of numbers and monads because the Good itself is the One (τὸ ἕν)" (*Eth. Eud.* 1218a). Likewise, in *Metaph.* 1.6, Aristotle explains that Plato teaches that the Ideas are the cause

truly is" (τὸ κατὰ τοῦτον ὄντως ὄν), which is a Platonic concept (*De E* 393a).[12] From the oneness of God the conclusion follows that God is incomposite. He writes, "For the Deity is not several, as each one of us is, made up out of an infinite number of different things in conditions of existence" (*De E* 393b).[13] Presupposing that the traditional gods are aspects of the one Deity, he interprets the name Apollo etymologically to mean Not-Many. He writes, "For 'Apollo,' inasmuch as it means 'denying many,' signifies also 'rejecting plurality.'" Likewise Apollo is also called Ἰήιος,[14] which Plutarch explains as implying divine oneness. Etymologically he derives the term Ἰήιος from the archaic ἴα, ἴης meaning one, being the equivalent of μία (*De E* 393b).[15] Similarly, he interprets the divine pair of Isis and Osiris as representing the two neo-Pythagorean principles of the monad and dyad (*Is.* 382c-e). The monad is said to be represented by the robe of Osiris, which is described as having "no shading or variety in its color, but only one simple (ἁπλοῦν) color like to light." Osiris's monochromatic robe symbolizes the undifferentiated first principle (ἀρχή), which is described as combined with nothing else (ἄκρατον). It is also called the first (τὸ πρῶτον), said to be without admixture (ἀμιγὲς) and to be intellectual (νοητόν) (382c-d). The reason that Plato and Aristotle call philosophy epoptic (mystic) is said to be because it concerns itself with "that primary, simple, and immaterial (principle),"[16] which is said to be the equivalent of making contact simply with the pure truth abiding about it (382e). Plutarch also identifies God with the Good (*Def. Or.* 423d).[17] It should also be noted, however, that Plutarch posits the existence of another god or demon responsible for the sublunary world, the realm of generation and decay (*De E* 398a-c).[18]

---

of all things and that the One is the cause of the Ideas. He writes, "Plato, then, declared himself thus on the points in question; it is evident from what has been said that he has used only two causes, that of the essence (τί ἐστιν) and the material cause or the Ideas are the causes of the essence of all other things, and the One (τὸ ἕν) is the cause of the essence of the Ideas" (988a).

12. See *Phaed.* 249c: εἰς τὸ ὂν ὄντως.

13. οὐ γὰρ πολλὰ τὸ θεῖόν ἐστιν, ὡς ἡμῶν ἕκαστος ἐκ μυρίων διαφορῶν ἐν πάθεσι γινομένων.

14. Meaning "archer" or derived from the cry used to invoke Apollo—ἰή.

15. Babbitt, *Plutarch. Moralia* V, 246, n.b.

16. πρὸς τὸ πρῶτον ἐκεῖνο καὶ ἁπλοῦν καὶ ἄυλον.

17. ἀγαθὸς γὰρ ὢν τελέως.

18 See Dillon, *The Middle Platonists*, 191.

Probably influenced by Plato's dialogue *Parmenides* (137c–139b), Albinus (Alcinous) argues in *Didaskalikos* that the primary God is without parts (ἀμέρης).[19] He holds that God cannot be a part of something, nor can he be a whole that has parts (10.4).[20] He explains later that the reason that God is without parts is that there can be nothing prior to God (10.7). If God had parts, then the parts would pre-exist God, the composite of which they are parts. For this reason God would no longer be the cause of all things. Being without parts means that God is incorporeal, since bodies consist of matter and form and therefore cannot be simple and primordial, as God is. Earlier Albinus (Alcinous) clarifies that the several attributes of God that he lists are not truly discrete. He writes, "I am not listing these terms as being distinct from one another, but on the assumption that one single thing is being denoted by all of them" (10.3). If he is truly without parts, then God cannot even have incorporeal attributes as parts or aspects of himself.

Under the influence of middle Platonism, Philo of Alexandria concludes that the Hebrew Bible's claim that God is one implies in addition that God is simple or incomposite.[21] In agreement with Scripture, he holds that God is numerically one, but he goes further in his reflections on divine oneness to include in it simplicity or incompositeness.[22] In an interpretation of what it means to be "alone" (μόνος) based on Gen 2:18, he asserts

19. Dillon, *Alcinous. The Handbook of Platonism*, 108, 110.

20. Dillon, *The Middle Platonists*, 139–83; Carabine, *The Unknown God*, 71–83.

21. On Philo, see Winston, "Philo's Conception of the Divine Nature," 21–41; Carabine, *The Unknown God*, 191–221; Frick, *Divine Providence in Philo of Alexandria*; Borgen, *Philo of Alexandria: An Exegete for his Time*; Calabi, *God's Acting, Man's Acting: Tradition and Philosophy in Philo of Alexandria*, 17–38.

22. According to Philo, the fourth of the five lessons that Moses teaches in the book of Genesis is that the cosmos is one because God is one (Runia, *Philo of Alexandria, On the Creation of the Cosmos according to Moses*, 391–403). He writes, "And fourth that the cosmos also that was thus created is one, since also the creator is one, and he, making his work resemble himself in its unity" (τέταρτον δ' ὅτι καὶ εἷς ἐστιν ὁ κόσμος, ἐπειδὴ καὶ εἷς ὁ δημιουργὸς <ὁ> ἐξομοιώσας αὐτῷ κατὰ τὴν μόνωσιν τὸ ἔργον) (*Opif.* 171). He is no doubt alluding to Plato's argument in *Timaeus* for the unity of the cosmos based on the unity of its model (*Tim.* 31a–b). Philo further explains by way of summary that "God is and exists, and that he who is is truly one" (καὶ ὅτι ἔστι καὶ ὑπάρχει θεὸς καὶ ὅτι εἷς ὁ ὢν ὄντως ἐστὶ) (172). The statement that God is the one who is (ὁ ὢν) is an interpretation of the name of God in Exod 3:14. God's oneness is a function of his unique being and is for that reason is truly one as opposed, presumably, to the lesser oneness of the cosmos. He also expresses God's oneness by referring to God as containing all things but being contained by nothing (*Leg.* 1.44; see *Migr.* 182, 192; *Post.* 6–17; *Somn.* 1.63–64; *Sobr.* 63; *Post.* 14; *Fug.* 75).

that God's oneness means God's uniqueness and incomparability: "But God, being one, is alone and one, and like God there is nothing" (οὐδὲν δὲ ὅμοιον θεῷ) (*Leg.* 2.1). God was alone before the creation of all things and after their creation nothing is ranked as the same as God, who is in need of nothing. If nothing is like him, then God cannot be known univocally; at best, God is analogous to things known in human experience.[23] There is, however, another interpretation provided for why it is appropriate for God to be alone: "God is alone and one, not composite, a simple nature" (*Leg.* 2.2).[24] In elucidation of this, Philo describes what God is not, in contrast to created beings: "But God is not composite, nor made up of many parts, but is without mixture with anything else" (*Leg.* 2.2).[25] He interprets God's oneness not only in a numerical sense, as in the Hebrew Bible, but also as denoting God's simplicity or incomposite nature, an absolute oneness. The reason that God is incomposite and therefore categorizable only according to the one and the monad (κατὰ τὸ ἕν καὶ τὴν μονάδα), which is to say, unique, is that whatever could be combined with God must be superior, equal, or inferior to God. But there is nothing superior or equal to God, and nothing inferior to God could be combined with God without diminishing him (*Leg.* 2.3). Philo also calls God a monad in the sense of being indivisible: "who knows no mixture or infusion and is in his isolation a monad" (καὶ κατὰ τὴν μόνωσιν μονάδι) (*Her.* 183; see *Spec.* 2.176; *Exod.* ii.68, 93). To be a monad is the opposite of being a composite. He further explains that the created monad resembles God insofar as it is incapable of addition or subtraction (*Her.* 187; *Spec.* 3.180). Drawing upon Pythagoreanism, he refers to God as "superior to the Good, more simple than the One and more ancient than the Monad" (*Contempl.* 1[2]); see *Deus* 82–83; *Praem.* 40).[26] In his view, God is greater than the Good and is more one and simple than both the One and the Monad, the origin of the One. God is not identified with the Good or the Monad but precedes both (see *Exod.* ii. 37 "simpler than the [number] one"). As one (and simple), God is said to be without qualities (ἄποιον αὐτὸν εἶναι), in addition to being imperishable and unchangeable (*Leg.* 1.51). Philo connects his theological assertion with

---

23. God is also said to be the one who *is* (τὸ ὄν), which is an allusion to Exod 3:14.

24. ὁ θεὸς μόνος ἐστι', καὶ ἕν, οὐ σύγκριμα, φύσις ἁπλῆ. See Wolfson, *Philo: Foundations of Religious Philosophy in Judaism, Christianity and Islam*, 1.171–73.

25. ὁ δὲ θεὸς, οὐ σύγκριμα, οὐδὲ ἐκ πολλῶν συνεστώς, ἀλλ' ἀμιγὴς ἄλλῳ

26. ὃ καὶ ἀγαθοῦ κρεῖττόν καὶ ἑνὸς εἰλικρινέστερον καὶ μονάδος ἀρχεγονώτερον

the biblical prohibition against making of idols: he extrapolates from this to include any depiction of God's qualities, including his incorporeal qualities. Being without qualities follows from being simple: what is truly one cannot have predicates because, if it did, a distinction could be made between it and what it is, in which case it would no longer be one (*Leg.* 1.44).[27]

In his work *Peri Tagathou*, as quoted by Eusebius in his *Praeparatio Evangelica* (11.17), the neo-Pythagorean Numenius of Apamea claims, "For he [the first God] is always simple and unchangeable" (ἁπλοῦν καὶ ἀναλλοίωτον) (frag. 6). Along the same lines, he affirms that the first God is eternally unchanging: "Being never was, nor ever became; but it always is in definite time." He then adds, "The first God, who exists in himself, is simple; for as he absolutely deals with none but himself, he is in no way divisible" (frag. 11).[28] For the first God to exist in himself (ἐν ἑαυτῷ ὤν) refers to his independence from all things, whereas his simplicity refers to his incompositeness, which is also expressed by affirming that the first God is not divisible (μὴ ποτε εἶναι διαιρετός). In this context, what it means for the first God to be simple is provided by the explanatory clause "for as he completely deals with none but himself" (διὰ τὸ ἑαυτῷ συγγιγόμενος διόλου). The meaning seems to be that the first God has nothing to which to relate, including his own attributes, which would thereby give him plurality. As simple, he is necessarily unchangeable since change presupposes composition. The first God is contrasted with the second God, who, although one like the first God, is brought into contact with matter, which is duality (dyad). Numenius obscurely states, "But in the process of coming into contact with matter, which is the dyad, he gives unity to it, but is himself divided by it" (frag. 11). The point is that the second God associates with matter, identified as the dyad in Pythagoreanism, for the purpose of bringing the (unified) cosmos into existence by imposing order on it. Contact with matter, however, results in his being divided from himself and so he is no longer simple. For this reason, the second God is called double (διττός), by which is meant plural (see frag. 16). It is explained that "the first God busies himself with the intelligible, while the second one deals with the intelligible and the

---

27. See *Migr.* 182, 192; *Post.* 6–17; *Somn.* 1.63–64; *Sobr.* 63; *Fug.* 75.

28. ὁ θεὸς ὁ μὲν πρῶτος ἐν ἑαυτῷ ὤν ἐστιν ἁπλοῦς, διὰ τὸ ἑαυτῷ συγγιγόμενος διόλου μὴ ποτε εἶναι διαιρετός. See Guthrie, *Numenius of Apamea. The Father of Neo-Platonism*, 115; Radde-Gallwitz, *The Transformation of Divine Simplicity*, 34–35. On Numenius, see Stead, *Divine Substance*, 186–87; Carabine, *The Unknown God*, 92–102; Dillon, *The Middle Platonists*, 361–79.

perceptible. . . . I call that characteristic of the first God, a standing still (στάσιν)" (frag. 21). Likewise, he claims ignorance of the name of the incorporeal, by which he means the first God; he does consent to call the first God being (οὐσία) and existence (ὄν) and describes him as simple and unchangeable: "The reason of this name 'Existent' is that he neither arose nor decayed, and admits of no motion whatever, nor any change to better or worse; for he is always simple (ἁπλοῦν) and unchangeable, and in the same idea, and does not abandon his identity either voluntarily, or compulsorily" (frag. 6). To be simple and unchanging are necessary correlates, as previously explained. Numenius also refers to the first God as mind (ὁ νοῦς), the creator of essence (ὁ τῆς οὐσίας δημιουργός), as well as the Good (τὸ ἀγαθόν) and the Good itself (αὐτοαγαθόν) (frag. 16). He also reiterates Plato's view that the Good is the One (frag. 19).

An explicitly Christianized but heretical version of the view that a perfect God, who is simple, is to be distinguished from a second God, who is the creator, is found in Ptolemy's *Letter to Flora* (found in Epiphanius, *Against Heresies*, 33.3.1—33.7.10), which may bear the influence of Numenius.[29] In discussing the question of the Law—its origin and nature—Ptolemy concludes with a discourse on the nature of the God who gave the Law.[30] The Law-giver is the creator (ὁ δημιουργός), but is distinguished from "the perfect God" (ὁ τέλειος θεός) (V.2) and from the devil (ὁ διάβολος). Fittingly, this God is said to be inferior to the perfect God and is given the name of intermediate (τὸ τῆς μεσότητος ὄνομα) (V.3). The creator is generated (γεννητός) (V.5) and therefore is different in essence from the perfect God (and also the devil) (V.3), who is ingenerate (ἀγέννητος) (V.5) and said to be the "one first principle of all" (μία ἀρχὴ τῶν ὅλων) (V.9). All things ultimately originate from the perfect God, even the creator, which is why the perfect God is identified as "Father of the whole" (πατὴρ τῶν ὅλων) (V.7). Based on Mark 10:18 "No one is good except God alone," the perfect God is said to be good by nature (ἀγαθός κατὰ τὴν ἑαυτοῦ φύσιν) (V.4), which reflects the traditional identification of God with the Platonic Good. The essence (οὐσία) of this God is further said to be "incorruption and self-existent light, simple and homogenous" (V.7).[31] The terms "simple" and "homogenous" are coordinate in meaning, since what is without composition is truly one thing. The fact that no argu-

---

29. Radde-Gallwitz, *The Transformation of Divine Simplicity*, 33–34.
30. Ibid., 31–37.
31. ἀφθαρσία τε φῶς αὐτοόν, ἁπλοῦν τε καὶ μονοειδές.

ment is offered for the simplicity of the perfect God implies that none is thought to be necessary: it is a commonplace assumption that the divine is simple. A better understanding of what it means for the perfect God to be simple can be obtained from contrasting him with the creator, whose essence (οὐσία) is said to have produced a double power (διττὴν μέν τινα δύναμιν) (V.8). Alluding to the account of creation in *Timaeus* (27d–30c), Ptolemy describes the origin of the cosmos on the assumption that the creator is not the perfect God, identical to the Good (*Tim.* 29e). The double power denotes the twofold relation that the intermediate God as creator has to the intelligible and material realms.[32] This twofold relation resulting in the twofold power means that the creator is not simple.

In Neoplatonism, the One and the Good is said to be simple. The neoplatonic philosopher Plotinus asserts that the nature of the Good (τἀγαθόν) is simple and first (ἁπλῆ ... καὶ πρώτη) (2.9.1).[33] Since it is the One (τὸ ἕν), the Good contains nothing beyond itself, for otherwise it would not be a unity.[34] It is explained that the designations the One and the Good are not predicates belonging to a subject, but are terms used to describe "the identical nature" (ἡ φύσις ἡ αὐτή), by which is meant identical *to itself*; this implies its incompositeness. Plotinus adds that the One is called the first only for the purpose of affirming that it is absolutely simple (ἁπλούστατον). Similarly, it is called self-sufficient (τὸ αὔταρκες) because it is not formed from a composite (οὐκ ἐκ πλειόνων). If it were, the One would depend upon parts and so would not be the first (τὸ πρῶτόν). For this reason, Plotinus says that the One is not "in another" (ἐν ἄλλῳ) and so is self-contained, because everything in another is from another (παρ ἄλλου), in the sense of being dependent on another. He concludes, "If therefore being from nothing other, and being in nothing other, in no way a composite, there can be nothing above it."[35] The one cannot be both a composite and the first, since its component parts would be ontologically

---

32. Matter is associated with the adversary, by which is mean the devil, whose nature is corruption and darkness, insofar as he is material and complex (ὑλικὸς ... πολυσχεδής) (V.6).

33. Gerson, *Plotinus*; Corrigan, *Reading Plotinus: A Practical Introduction to Neoplatonism*, chap. 3; Hines, *Return to the One*, 35–81; Cooper, *Panentheism: The Other God of the Philosophers*, 39–43.

34. καὶ τὸ πρῶτον δὲ οὕτως, ὅτι ἁπλούστατον, καὶ τὸ αὔταρκες. ὅτι οὐκ ἐκ πλειόνων.

35. εἰ οὖν μηδὲ παρ ἄλλου μηδὲ ἐν ἄλλῳ μηδὲ σύνωεσις μηδεμία, ἀνάγκη μηδὲν ὑπὲρ αὐτὸ εἶναι.

before it. The same argument is found elsewhere in the *Enneads*: "For to this self-sufficient, to which nothing can be connected. This self-sufficing is the essence of its unity" (6.9.6).[36] Plotinus argues that plurality presupposes unity that is first, simple and self-sufficient, serving as the source of plurality.[37] It follows that the One is infinite (ἄπειρον) in the sense that it cannot be determined to be anything, since to assign a predicate to the One would be to introduce duality into it (6.9.6).[38] Similarly, he asserts that the One as simple, having no multiplicity (σύνθεσις), is before all things and is the ineffable source (ἀρχή) of them. For this reason it cannot be a body (σῶμα), because a body is not simple (5.4.1). Because it has no parts, the One has no distinctiveness: neither pattern nor form (οὐδὲ σχῆμα ... οὐδὲ μορφή) (5.5.11); what is simple cannot have properties that express how it is distinct from what it is not. Plotinus denies not only movement but also rest to the One because to say that the One is at rest is to repudiate its simplicity insofar as rest would be a property of the One (6.9.3).[39] Likewise intellection cannot even be ascribed to the One, not even self-knowledge, since a distinction would be made between essence and the act of intellection. As a result, the One would cease to be simple because something has been added to it, namely intellection (6.7.37).[40]

Like Plotinus, the neoplatonic philosopher Proclus considers the One and Good to be simple. He argues that the One and Good is self-sufficient, by which is meant that it is itself in the sense of being independent of all things for its existence (*Instit. theol.* prop. 41). He then concludes that whatever is self-sufficient is simple insofar as, if composite, it would be constituted by and depend on its parts and so not be self-sufficient (*Instit. theol.* prop. 47).

---

36. ἐφ᾿ ἑαυτοῦ γὰρ ἐστιν οὐδενὸς αὐτῷ συμβεβηκότος. τῷ αὐτάρκει δ ἄν τις καὶ τὸ ἓν αὐτοῦ ἐνθυμηθείη.

37. δεῖ μὲν γάρ τι πρὸ πάντων εἶναι.

38. See Meijer, *Plotinus on the Good or the One (Enneads VI, 9): An Analytical Commentary.*

39. ὥστε συμβήσεται αὐτῷ καὶ οὐκέτι ἁπλοῦν μενεῖ—ἁπλοῦν τοῦτο—καὶ πάντων ἕτερον τῶν μετ᾿ αὐτό, ἐφ᾿ ἑαυτοῦ ὄν, οὐ μεμιγμένον τοῖς ἀπ᾿ αὐτοῦ.

40. Plotinus explains the relation of the νοῦς to the One: "What now has engendered this God, what is the simplex (ὁ ἁπλοῦς) preceding this multiple; what the cause at once of its existence and of its existing as a manifold; what the source of this Number, this Quantity? Number, Quantity, is not primal: obviously before even duality, there must stand the unity" (*Enn.* 5.1.5).

God as Simple in Christian Theology

Until the modern period, Christian theologians almost unanimously assert that there is another, more fundamental type of oneness attributable to God than numerical oneness.[41] God is one not only in the sense of being unique, but also one in the sense of being simple or non-composite: God has no constituent parts.[42] Although the church does not establish it as a dogma until the Fourth Lateran Council in 1215, nevertheless theologians affirm the simplicity doctrine from the beginning.[43] There is no shortage of expressions of it. Clement of Alexandria, for example, asserts without argumentation, "Nor are any parts to be predicated of him. For the One is indivisible" (*Strom.* 5.12.32).[44] Likewise Origen affirms apodictically, "Now God is altogether one and simple" (*Comm. Jn.* 1.20.119).[45] According to him, for God to be one is to be simple. Augustine claims that God can be defined by twelve attributes: "eternal, immortal, incorruptible, unchangeable, living, wise, powerful, beautiful, righteous, good, blessed spirit" (*De Trin.* XV.8).[46] Of these twelve, he says that only the last signifies substance, the other eleven being qualities. What he means is that to define God as a "blessed spirit" is to say that he is a substance or a thing, whereas to define him as eternal or wise, for example, is to attribute a quality to that substance. Augustine insists, however, that the distinction between quality and substance actually does not apply in the case of "that ineffable and simple nature" (*De Trin.* XV.8).[47] Because it is not something different for God to be and to be something, insofar as God is necessary, whatever is attributed to God is always according to substance and not according to quality: "For whatever seems to be predicated therein according to quality (*secundum qualitates*), is to be understood according to substance or

---

41. See Oden, *The Living God: Systematic Theology: Volume One*, 57–58; Rogers, "The Traditional Doctrine of Divine Simplicity," 166.

42. The most common word in Greek used is ἁπλοῦς and in Latin simplex, but other terms are also used.

43. The Fourth Lateran Council states that God is an "altogether simple substance or nature" (*substantia seu natura simplex omnino*). This is reiterated centuries later at the First Vatican Council: God is said to be "wholly simple" (*simplex omnino*).

44. οὐδὲ μὴν μέρη τινὰ αὐτοῦ λεκτέον· ἀδιαίρετον γὰρ τὸ ἕν. See Radde-Gallwitz, *The Transformation of Divine Simplicity*, 51–59.

45. ὁ θεὸς μὲν οὖν πάντῃ ἕν ἐστι καὶ ἁπλοῦν.

46. Teske, "Properties of God and the Predicaments in De Trinitate V," 4–5.

47. Illa ineffabili simplicique natura.

essence (*secundum substantiam vel essentiam*)" (*De Trin.* XV.8). In so doing, Augustine denies that God has true qualities. Along the same lines, Anselm asserts that the divine attributes are not parts of God because God's oneness implies that God is not "capable of dissolution even in thought" (*nullo intellectu divisibilis*) (*Pros.* 18). Although there are some dissenters, virtually all Christian theologians until the modern period include the simplicity doctrine as a central part of their treatment of God, in particular as what distinguishes God from created beings.

The simplicity doctrine is assumed by Protestantism in spite of its biblicism and critical stance towards the overly-speculative tendencies of medieval scholasticism. Lutheran and Reformed theologians are indistinguishable from their medieval predecessors in this regard, arguing for the simplicity of God against Socinians, Remonstrants, such as Vorstius, and Arminians.⁴⁸ As the Lutheran Johannes Wollebius succinctly explains, "Simplicity is where God is understood as a being that is truly one without any composition."⁴⁹ He, like others, uses the phrase ὅλως ὅλον (*totaliter totum*) to describe God's simplicity, by which is meant that God is a whole without parts.⁵⁰ While angels and human souls are thought to be relatively simple as compared to corporeal things, God is absolutely simple, insofar as God admits of no composition whatsoever. According to Reformed theologian Francis Turretin, the doctrine of God's simplicity includes not only the assertion that God is "free from all composition and division," but also that God is "incapable of composition and divisibility."⁵¹ God is such that he cannot be otherwise than simple; this is one respect in which God is limited by his own nature because not to be simple is not to be God. Thus two senses of the oneness of God are to be distinguished: *unitas singularitatis* and *unitas simplicitatis*, or God as *unio* which excludes rival gods and God as *unitas*, which excludes composition.⁵² Combining Deut 6:4 "The

---

48. Heppe, *Reformed Dogmatics*, 63–65. See Hampton, *Anti-Arminians*, 192–220.

49. Simplicitas est, qua Deus ens vere Unum omnisque compositionis expers intelligitur. *Compendium Theologiae Christianae*, lib. 1, cap. 1.

50. Or, as Heidegger more exhaustively expresses it, "Simplicitas Dei est, per quam is omnis compositionis, coalitionis, concretionis, commixtionis, confusionis & diversitatis expers ita est, ut quicquid in Deo et cogitatur, ipse Deus sit, adeoque essentiae Divinae et attributorum, atque etiam attributorum inter se absolutissima identitas sit" (*Corpus theologiae christianae* Locus tertius xxxii).

51. Incapax componibilitatis et divisibilitatis. Turretin, *Institutio Theologiae Elencticae*, locus tertius, quaest. VII. III.

52. Some later versions of the simplicity doctrine lose the precision that earlier

LORD, our God, is one LORD" with Ps 102:27 "Thou art the same," Puritan theologian John Owen draws the conclusion that God is "one and the same," by which is meant that God has no composition; this is what Exod 3:14-15 and Rev 1:8 are said to affirm (*Vind.* XII.72). He concludes, "He, then, who is what he is, and whose all that is in him is, himself, hath neither parts, accidents, principles nor anything else, whereof his essence should be compounded." The simplicity doctrine is even incorporated into Protestant Confessions of Faith, which are intended for use by lay people. The Westminster Confession and the Thirty-Nine Articles of the Church of England both state that God is "without body, parts, or passions." Similarly, the Belgic Confession refers to God as *"une seule et simple essence"* (art. 1).

As used by Christian theologians, the simplicity doctrine has had both a polemical function and a dogmatic one. Polemically, it has been used as a weapon against certain heretical views, in particular Gnosticism and Arianism.[53] In such cases, the assertion of God's simplicity serves as a means to the end of repudiating theological proposals considered unacceptable. Against the Gnostics it is argued that one cannot conceive God as having emanations (aeons) that have a quasi-independent ontological status, since God is not a composite being. According to Irenaeus, Gnostics such as Valentinus naively assume that God is like human beings in having "the affections, and passions, and mental tendencies of human beings" (*Adv. Haer.* 2.13.3), and then hypostatize these to become the triacontad, the thirty aeons that emanated from God, also known as Buthos among other designations. In refutation of the Gnostic concept of God, Irenaeus asserts that God the Father is "a simple, uncompounded being, without diverse members, and altogether like, and equal to himself" (*Adv. Haer.* 2.13.3; see 1.15.5).[54] God as simple means that God has no parts, but is wholly everything that one may legitimately predicate of him. Because of this, Irenaeus judges that the Valentinian idea of the pleroma is philosophically naïve.[55]

---

expressions of the doctrine have, e.g., Shedd, *Dogmatic Theology*, 1.338-39.

53. See Irenaeus, *Adv. Haer.* 2.13.3, 5; 2.28.4-5; Athanasius, *Decr.*11, 22; *Adv. gent.* 3.41; *Ep. Afr.*; Hilary, *De Trin.* 5.26; 8.43; 9.61; Gregory of Nyssa, *Con. Eunom.* 1.1.232, 237; 2.1.475; 2.1.483, 487; 2.1.557; 3.10.46-48; *Abl.*; Ambrose, *De fide* 1.16.106.

54. On Irenaeus, see Lawson, *The Biblical Theology of Saint Irenaeus*; Grant, *Irenaeus of Lyons*, chap. 3; Osborn, *Irenaeus of Lyons*, chap. 3; Minns, *Irenaeus: An Introduction*, chap. 3.

55. Irenaeus claims to find this view in Scripture: "But if they had known the scriptures ... they would have known ... that God is not as men are; and that his thoughts are

The Oneness and Simplicity of God

In the Arian controversy, the simplicity of God is used in different ways in support of orthodoxy. From what Athanasius writes, the Arians themselves use divine simplicity in support of their Christology. In particular, they argue that the Son cannot be the proper offspring (τὸ ἴδιον γέννημα) of the essence of the Father since this would lead to the contradictory assertion that the simple God is divisible (*Ar.* 1.15).[56] Athanasius's response is that the Arians wrongly think of God the Father's generation of the Son on analogy with the generation of material things, which is impossible without the assumption of parts and divisions (χωρὶς τῆς ἐκ μερῶν καὶ διαιρέσεων). Rather, the generation of the Son is of a different order. In fact, in another work he turns the tables on the Arians by arguing that, because he is simple, God must always be a Father and so could not become a Father by adding to his essence fatherhood insofar as he begets the Son. He writes, "In naming 'God' and naming 'Father' we name nothing as if about him, but signify his essence" (*Decr.* 22; see *Ar.* 1.28; 2.34; 4.2). God is not Father by way of the addition of an accidental property to his essence, but is *essentially* Father: for God to be is to be Father.[57] It follows that God has always been Father, in which case the Son is eternally-begotten and has the same essence as the Father.[58] Similarly, on the basis of the simplicity of God, Athanasius concludes that the Word must be fully God, albeit begotten: "But God possesses true existence and is not composite, wherefore his Word also has true existence and is not composite, but is the one

---

not like the thoughts of men," which seems to be an amalgamation of Num 23:19 and Isa 55:8 (*Adv. Haer.* 2.13.3). From the premise that God is not like a human being, he draws the conclusion that, unlike human beings, God is incomposite.

56. Hough, *Athanasius: The Hero*, 143–56; Anatolius, *Athanasius*; Weinandy, *Athanasius: A Theological Introduction*, 49–80; Leithart, *Athanasius*, 57–88; Gwynn, *Anthanasius of Alexandria: Bishop, Theologian, Ascetic, Father*, 55–104.

57. As Athanasius explains, "If then any man conceives God to be compound, as accident is in essence (σύνθετον ὡς ἐν τῇ οὐσίᾳ τὸ συμβεβηκὸς)" (*Decr.* 22.1).

58. Likewise Athanasius writes, "If when you name the Father, or use the word 'God,' you do not signify essence, or understand him according to essence, who is that he is, but signify something else about him, not to say inferior, then you should not have written that the Son was from the Father, but from what is about him or in him; and so, shrinking from saying that God is truly Father, and making him compound who is simple, in a material way, you will be authors of a newer blasphemy. . . . But if, when we hear it said, 'I am that I am' (Exod 3:1) and, 'In the beginning God created the heaven and the earth' (Gen 1:1) and, 'Hear, O Israel, the Lord our God is one Lord' (Deut 6:4) and, 'Thus says the Lord Almighty', we understand nothing else than the very simple, and blessed, and incomprehensible essence itself of him that is" (*De syn.* 34–35). See Gregory of Nyssa, *Con. Eunom.* 1.1.597–98.

and only-begotten God (John 1:18)" (*Adv. gent.* 41.1; see 28.3 3; *Ep. Afr.* 8).[59] Hilary likewise uses the idea of divine simplicity to refute Arianism.[60] Exegeting John 5, he argues that, if the Father has life in himself and has given the Son to have life in himself (5:26), then the Son must share a common (simple) nature with the Father.[61] This is because "God is not after human fashion of a composite being (*ex compositis*), so that in him there is a difference of kind between possessor and possessed" (*De Trin.* 8.43). In other words, God cannot give something distinct from himself (i.e., life) to the Son but must give himself: "For when he says that he has what the Father has, he means that he has the Father's self" (*De Trin.* 8.43).

Basil also employs the simplicity doctrine to defend Trinitarianism against Arianism. Responding to the accusation of his opponents that he and his supporters are tritheists, he insists that his understanding of God as simple precludes such a possibility (*Ep.* 8). In his view, God is one in a more fundamental sense than numerically (τῷ ἀριθμῷ): God is "one really" (ἓν ὄντως), which is identical to being one in nature (ἓν τῇ φύσει). To be one in nature is to be simple (ἁπλοῦν) and incomposite (ἀσύνθετος) (8.2).[62] He cites examples of things that can be numerically one but not one in nature, such as the world, a human being and even an angel. It is not that he is contradicting the biblical confession that there is one God. Rather, when

---

59. This argument is later repeated by Ambrose. Rejecting the Arian identification of being begotten with being created, he argues that Christ could not be created because being created in the sense of coming from God would mean that something is added to the nature of God. But this is impossible, since God is simple: "Moreover, how can there be any created nature in God? In truth, God is of a simple nature, not combined or composed (*naturae simplicis est, non conjunctae atque compositae*); nothing can be added to him, and that alone which is divine has he in his nature" (*De fide* 1.16.106). The only theological option is to posit another type of being begotten, i.e. eternally begotten.

60. According to Hilary, Arius uses divine simplicity to prove that the Son was made from nothing, for otherwise the Son would have been made from God, which contradicts the simplicity of God. He quotes from Arius's *Letter to Alexander of Alexandria*: "As to such phrases as from him, and from the womb, and I went out from the Father and have come, if they be understood to denote that the Father extends a part and, as it were, a development of that one substance, then the Father will be of a compound nature (*compositus*) and divisible and changeable and corporeal, according to them; and thus, as far as their words go, the incorporeal God will be subjected to the properties of matter" (*De Trin.* 6.4) (see also Athanasius, *De syn.* 16). If God the Father begets the Son from himself then God must be composite and divisible.

61. See Borchardt, *Hilary of Poitiers' Role in the Arian Struggle*; Weedman, *The Trinitarian Theology of Hilary of Poitiers*.

62. It is argued that the author was actually Evagrius Ponticus (Sr Agnes Clare Way, C.D.P., trans., *St. Basil: Letters: vol. 1*, 21–40).

The Oneness and Simplicity of God

he says that God is not numerically one he means not *merely* numerically one, but rather one in nature and therefore *necessarily* numerically one. This eliminates the possibility of tritheism. Instead of numerically one, Basil prefers to refer to God as monad and unity: "Monad and oneness on the other hand signify the nature which is simple and incomprehensible" (*Ep.* 8.2).[63] Finally, Gregory of Nyssa takes aim at Eunomius's view of the gradations of the divine nature, arguing that on the assumption of divine simplicity there can be no such degrees of deity among the three persons of the Trinity.[64] He writes, "We comprehend a power without parts (ἀμερῆ) and without composition (ἀσύνθετον); how then, and on what grounds, could anyone perceive there any differences of less and more?" (*Con. Eunom.* 1.1.232; see 1.1.237; 2.1.557). From this it should follow that the Son cannot be inferior to the Father, as Eunomius assumes. Rather, since God is simple, whatever God begets must be fully God.[65]

Yet one should not explain adherence to the simplicity doctrine as resulting merely from polemical expediency, as a means of combatting heresy. Rather, from the beginning of Christian theology the simplicity doctrine has been dogmatically affirmed in its own right.[66] It has an unassailable place in the church's theological self-expression. John of Damascus defines a compound (σύνθετον) as "that which is composed of many and different things" (*O.F.* 1.9). The parts in a compound are any discrete

---

63. ἡ δὲ μονὰς καὶ ἑνὰς τῆς ἁπλῆς καὶ ἀπεριλήπτου οὐσίας ἐστὶ σημαντική. See *Adv. Eunom.* 2.29.

64. See Meredith, *Gregory of Nyssa*, 27–58; Vaggione, *Eunomius of Cyzicus and the Nicene Revolution*; Radde-Gallwitz, *The Transformation of Divine Simplicity*, 175–224.

65. Gregory of Nyssa describes God by the phrase "simple and incomposite" (τὸν ἁπλοῦν καὶ ἀσύνθετον) (*Con. Eunom.* 1.1.683), and makes reference to the simplicity (ἁπλότης) of God (*Con. Eunom.* 3.10.48). He also refers to God as being "one good in a simple and uncompounded nature" (ἀγαθὸν ἐν ἁπλῇ τε καὶ ἀσυνθέτῳ τῇ φύσει) (*Con. Eunom.* 3.1.125), as "what is incorporeal and immaterial, simple, and without figure" (τὸ ἀσώματόν τε καὶ ἄϋλον ἁπλοῦν τε καὶ ἀσχημάτιστον) (*Con. Eunom.* 3.1.128) and speaks of the "life that is divine, simple, and immaterial" (τῆς θείας καὶ ἁπλῆς καὶ ἀΰλου ζωῆς) (*Con. Eunom.* 3.2.4; see 3.10). In his dispute with Eunomius, he assumes that his opponent agrees that God is a "simple and uncompounded essence" (τὴν ἁπλῆν τε καὶ ἀσύνθετον οὐσίαν) (*Con. Eunom.* 3.8.7), "who is by nature simple, uncompounded, and indivisible" (ὁ γὰρ ἁπλοῦν τῇ φύσει καὶ ἀμερὲς καὶ ἀσύθετον) (*Con. Eunom.* 3.8.48). He states axiomatically that everyone would agree that God as simple, being "viewless, formless, and sizeless, cannot be conceived of as multiform and composite (πολυειδῆ καὶ σύνθετον)" (*Con. Eunom.* 1.1.131). The point of contention between him and Eunomius concerns whether the Son is likewise.

66. Stead, *Divine Substance*, 163–65; 186–89.

predicates—even negations—that can be attributed to a subject, in this case God. To use modern philosophical terminology, these predicates express properties.[67] What is incompatible with divine simplicity is any conception that distinguishes one or more part of God, which is to say, properties that are instantiated in God. Often with the aid of Aristotelian ontology, modes of compositeness are enumerated, each of which is then denied of God. It is true to say, however, that there is a certain amount of equivocation that occurs with respect to the discussion of divine simplicity. Predicates expressing properties of God are sometimes tacitly assumed to be generically the same insofar as grammatically they are predicates. In addition, there is a tendency to understand non-physical predicates expressing attributes or properties on analogy with the physical type.[68]

The most obvious type of composition that God lacks is that resulting from having or being a body.[69] What exactly is meant by having or being a body, however, is often not fully explained.[70] In more modern versions of it, a common sense or phenomenological understanding of the body is often assumed.[71] In earlier versions, a Platonic or Aristotelean view is used, according to which the body is informed matter, characterized by mutability.[72] Because God has or is no body, which is expressed also by saying that God is incorporeal, it follows that God is devoid of quantitatively-distinct, physical parts existing as spatially separated from one another, which is true of bodies.[73] For Aristotelian-influenced theologians an extension of

---

67. William Vallicella differentiates two types of properties: "a property of x as a constituent of x, or as an entity external to x to which x is tied by the asymmetrical relation (or nonrelational tie) of instantiation" ("Divine Simplicity").

68. See Bennett, "The Divine Simplicity"; Hughes, *Complex Theory*, 29–30.

69. See Wainwright, "God's Body."

70. For a summary of types of compositeness, see Dolezal, *God without Parts*, 31–66.

71. Brian Davies writes, "To begin with, of course, we will have to deny that God is something bodily. Otherwise he will simply be part of the world of existence of which is said to depend on him in terms of the doctrine of creation" ("The Doctrine of Divine Simplicity," 60–61). What he needs to explain is what existing "bodily" means. Likewise he writes, "We distinguish between individuals in the world because they are material or because they exist in the context of materiality. . . . And in this sense we can deny that God is an individual" (62). What matter is, and why God is not material, however, is not provided. Rather a common sense or phenomenological view of matter is assumed.

72. Moreover, matter is an irreducible fact, being that which the five senses have for their object, and is marked by potentiality to receive the Intelligibles, the Ideas.

73. Ex partibus integrantibus seu quantitativis (Quenstedt, *Theologia didactico-polemica sive systema theologicum*, cap. VIII; sect. I, thesis XI).

the conclusion that God has or is not a body is that God is not composed of matter and form.[74] Rather, God is said to be pure form (*forma pura* or *forma purissima*).[75] Whether this makes sense even on Aristotelian presuppositions is a valid question, but at least Aristotle himself held this view.[76]

Other, less-obvious types of composition are also denied of God, which can be called instances of metaphysical compositeness, as opposed to the physical type.[77] First, presupposing an Aristotelian explanation of becoming, theologians have claimed that God does not consist of actuality and potentiality, which, if he did, would make God composite. Rather God is said to be pure act (*actus purus*), having no potentiality.[78] If God had potentiality then God could be distinguished from God's potentiality, what

---

74. On this topic, see Gilson, *Being and Some Philosophers*, 178; Chappell, "Aristotle's Conception of Matter." For an Aristotelian, matter is always the matter of a form, and does not exist separable from form.

75. See Aquinas, *ST* 1.3.2. Aquinas provides two other reasons for his view that God does not consist of matter and form. Second, whatever is composed of matter and form owes its perfection and goodness to form and not matter. What he means is that matter participates in form and so its goodness and perfection is participated. But God's goodness is not a participated goodness and so God cannot have matter, but must be form only. Third, he asserts that God does not consist of matter and form because every agent acts by its form and because God is the first agent in the sense of being the first efficient cause. It follows that God must be form only: "Therefore whatever is primarily and essentially an agent must be primarily and essentially form. Now God is the first agent, since he is the first efficient cause." Since God is not acted upon but is "primarily and essentially" an agent, God must be form only because whatever has matter by definition can be acted upon. He concludes that the essence of God is to be form and not to be composed of matter and form.

76. "But the first essence has no matter; for it is complete reality (τὸ δὲ τί ἦν εἶναι οὐκ ἔχει ὕλην τὸ πρῶτον· ἐντελέχεια γάρ) (*Metaph*. 12.8; 1074a 36–39)."

77. Morris identifies three types of compositeness: spatial (or physical), temporal and metaphysical complexity (*Our Idea of God*, 113–18; see also Morris, "Dependence and Divine Simplicity." He calls the third type property simplicity. Using modern terminology, he labels the lack metaphysical compositeness property simplicity because God exemplifies no properties distinct from himself, unlike all created things (*Our Idea of God*, 114–15). Of course, simplicity is not to be understood as the property of having no properties, but is rather "a name for the mysterious way in which the being of God supports our many true characterizations of him without ultimately being divisible into substance and attributes as are his creatures" (115). Morris does not agree with this view, being an advocate of perfect-being theology. See Mullins, "Simply Impossible: A Case against Divine Simplicity."

78. See Hughes, *The Nature of God: An Introduction to the Philosophy of Religion*, chap. 2; Burns, "The Status and Function of Divine Simpleness in *Summa Theologiae* Ia, qq. 2–13"; Lamont, "Aquinas on Divine Simplicity"; Weigel, *Aquinas on Simplicity*, 90–102; 103–35.

From God as Numerically One to God as Simple

God could be or do. Aquinas states, "In the first mover, which is altogether immobile, all combination of potency and act is impossible" (*Compend.* 1.9).[79] In this context, potentiality is conceived as being a part, on analogy to a physical part. The view that God as simple has no potentiality is a fixture of Christian theology, and carries over into Protestant scholasticism, although often without the explicit Aristotelian foundation. Lutheran theologian Johann Gerhard identifies seven types of composition that do not characterize God, including that consisting of act and potentiality (*ex actu et potentia*).[80] Likewise, Swiss Reformed theologian Johann Heidegger claims that God is exempt from any composition of act and potentiality. Citing Exod 3:14, Mal 3:6 and 1 Tim 1:17, he seeks to establish that God is incapable of change, which means in Aristotelian terms that God is pure act with no potentiality.[81] Most Protestant scholastics argue similarly.

Second, making use of Aristotelian categories, Christian theologians assert that God cannot be conceived compositely as being constituted by genus and differentia, or specific difference.[82] A species, defined by its differentia, exists potentially in its genus, but God as simple cannot consist of a genus and differentia, for otherwise God would have two parts. Moreover, not being in a genus follows from the lack of potentiality in God. God could not be in any genus as a species because this would mean that God would have potentiality insofar as he would be in his genus potentially. As Aquinas concludes, "Hence since in God actuality is not added to potentiality, it is impossible that he should be in any genus as a species" (*ST* 1.3.5).[83] Likewise Lutheran theologian Johannes Quenstedt identifies six types of composition from which God is exempt, the first of which is genus and differentia (*ex genere et differentia*).[84] (All of these modes of compositeness are true of human beings and some are true of angels.) He argues that God is exempt from any composition consisting of genus and differentia

---

79. In primo autem movente, si est omnino immobile, impossibile est esse potentiam cum actu.

80. Gerhard, *Loci theologici*, locus secundus, caput viii, sect. III §129.

81. Heidegger, *Corpus theologiae christianae*, locus tertius, xxxii.

82. Holloway differentiates between physical and logical parts. The former are not necessarily material but are components of a thing, whereas the latter relate to the definition and includes genus and species (*An Introduction to Natural Theology*, 231–34).

83. Unde, cum in Deo non adiungatur potentia actui, impossibile est quod sit in genere tanquam species.

84. Quenstedt, *Theologia didactico-polemica sive systema theologicum*, cap. VIII; sect. I, thesis XI; sect. II quaest. V.

because God is most pure act without potentiality. A species, defined by its differentia, exists potentially in its genus, which cannot be true of God as pure act. Finally, Johann Heidegger says that God is excluded *ex partibus universalibus*, by which he means genus and differentia. He interprets Deut 4:35 "Yahweh is God; besides him there is no other" to mean that God is one in the sense of not being composed of a genus and differentia.[85]

Third, it is claimed that, because God is simple, there cannot be in God any distinction between subject and accident (*ex subjecto et accidentibus*). In other words, whatever is in God is in the divine essence and so whatever is predicated of God can only be predicated essentially. Augustine draws the conclusion that God cannot have accidental qualities: "In the substance of God there is not anything of such a nature as would imply that therein substance is one thing, and that which is accident to substance (*aliud quod accidat substantiae*) another thing, and not substance" (*Fide et symb.* 9 [20]).[86] Because God "alone is properly and truly simple," Peter Lombard likewise concludes that in God there are no accidents and for that reason no mutability in God. He writes, "In the divine nature there is no diversity of accidents and no mutability throughout but rather a perfect simplicity" (*Sent.* I.8.7).[87] Along the same lines, Aquinas concludes from God's simplicity that there is nothing accidental in God, but rather that God's essence is the same as God. He writes, "In God, however, since he is simple . . . there are not found two things whereof one is *per se* and the other *per accidens*. Therefore his essence must be absolutely the same as he himself" (*Compend.* 1.10).[88] God is not anything accidentally, but can only be what he is essentially. Or, as the Lutheran scholastic theologian Amandus Polanus expresses it, "Whatever is predicated of God is predicated absolutely, that is, according to *ousia*, being understood essentially and not accidentally."[89]

---

85. Heidegger, *Corpus theologiae christianae*, locus tertius, xxxii.

86. La Croix does not seem fully to appreciate Augustine's position ("Augustine on the Simplicity of God"). See Teske, "Properties of God and the Predicaments in *De Trinitate* V."

87. Augustine explains that nothing can be predicated of God accidentally because there is nothing in God that can be changed or lost or that is capable of increase or decrease (*De Trin.* V. 5; see *Civ. Dei* 11.10).

88. In Deo autem, cum sit simplex, ut ostensum est, non est invenire duo quorum unum sit per se, et aliud per accidens. Oportet igitur quod essentia eius sit omnino idem quod ipse.

89. Polanus, *Syntagma theologiae Christianae*, lib. IIX, cap. X. Quicquid de Deo absolute praedicatur, id οὐσιωδῶς, id est essentialiter, non accidentaliter intelligitur." He adds as further explanation, "In Deum nullum cadit accidens, nec quicquam est in deo

From God as Numerically One to God as Simple

Fourth, not only is God as simple without accidents, but no distinction can be made between God as suppositum or subject and God's essence or nature. To do so would require composition in God, insofar as a distinction would be made between God and what God is, God's essence or nature. Even essential attributes can be distinguished from the suppositum or subject to which they belong; in the case of God, however, simplicity precludes this possibility. To eliminate the distinction between God as suppositum or subject and God's essence or nature is counterintuitive and leads to some very subtle theologizing. According to Gregory of Nyssa, contrary to Eunomius, even to say that God has only one essential attribute like ingenerateness would mean that God is composite insofar as God would consist of a suppositum or subject and that one predicate. So, in light of divine simplicity, the only appropriate name for God, in the sense of attribute, is "the name above every name" (Phil 2:9), which is to say no-name. Gregory's view is that God as simple is nameless *in principle*, not simply unnameable by human beings.[90]

Similarly, in the process of explaining the apparent distinction made in John 4:34 between the will of the Father and that of the Son, Cyril of Alexandria gives expression to the hermeneutical presupposition that any distinction made with respect to God, "the supreme nature" (ἡ ἀνωτάτω φύσις), even essential predication, is ultimately unreal. God may appear in Scripture to be composite, having attributes, but this is an accommodation to human limitation: human beings cannot understand a simple God, a fact that Cyril finds expressed by the apostle Paul's statement "we see in a mirror dimly" (1 Cor 13:12). The simple (ἁπλοῦς) God is spoken about in Scripture in human terms (ἀνθρωπίνως), as if he were a compound (διπλοῦς). On the same presupposition, Augustine affirms that the Trinity is simple because, "it is what it has" (*quod habet hoc est*) (*De Trin.* XI.10). The meaning of this terse, often-quoted theological statement is that God and God's essential qualities are identical, which further implies that God is necessary.[91] If one could make a distinction between

---

quod non sit per se.

90. See *Con. Eunom.* 1.1.683; 2.1.586–87; *Abl.* 3, 1.52; *In eccl.* 7.411.

91. Augustine also writes, "Those things which are essentially and truly divine are called simple, because in them quality and substance are not distinct, nor do they participate in any deity, wisdom or beatitude" (dicuntur illa simplicia, quae principaliter uereque divina sunt, quod non aliud est in eis qualitas, aliud substantia, nec aliorum participatione vel divina vel sapientia vel beata sunt) (*De Trin.* XI.10) (see VIII.6 "this unchangeableness and this simplicity"). Similarly, Anselm asserts, "Thus there are no parts in you, O Lord, nor are you many and not one: but you are one and the same with

43

The Oneness and Simplicity of God

God and that whereby God is God, then God would not be simple (see *De Trin.* 6.8; 7.2). Influenced by Augustine, Peter Lombard, writes "Moreover of this essence there is so great a simplicity and sincerity, that there is not in it anything that is not itself; but the same is the one having and what is had" (*Sent.* I. 8.8).[92] The idiomatic statement that with respect to God it is the same thing to have (*habens*) and be had (*quod habetur*) means that one cannot distinguish between God as subject and what is predicable of God, even essentially. Commenting on Lombard's *Sentences*, Bonaventure likewise argues that, because God is what God has, then God is simple: "Everything that is whatever it has, is most simple (*Comm. sent.* I. 7.2.1).[93] In other words, since there is no distinction between God's substance and God's qualities—or, expressed differently, between God as suppositum and as *natura*—then God is incomposite, not being composed of a substratum and its various essential qualities. Otherwise God would be God by virtue of his essential qualities and so would not be God because he would not be first.

Fifth, to affirm that God is simple is to affirm that there is no distinction in God between God's essence and existence (*essentia et existentia*).[94] With respect to everything other than God, a distinction can be made between a thing's essence and its existence; the former expresses *what* a thing is whereas the latter expresses *that* it is.[95] Such an assertion rests on the

---

yourself (*idem tibi ipsi*), so that in nothing are you unlike yourself; rather you are very oneness itself, indivisible by any understanding. Therefore life and wisdom and your other attributes are not parts of you but are all one, and every one of them is wholly what you are and what the other attributes are" (*Prosl.* 18). Likewise in his *Monologium*, he writes, "For since a man cannot be justice but can have justice, a just man is not understood to be a man who is justice but to be a man who has justice. So since the Supreme Nature is not properly said to have justice but rather to be justice, then when [this Nature] is said to be just, it is properly understood to be [a Nature] which is justice rather than to be [a Nature] which has justice. Hence, if when we say that it is [a Nature] which is justice we are saying not what kind of thing it is but rather what it is, then (by logical inference) when we say that it is just, we are saying not what kind of thing it is but what it is" (16).

92. Huius autem essentiae simplicitas ac sinceritas tanta est, quod non est in ea aliquid, quod non sit ipsa; sed idem est habens et quod habetur.

93. Omne quod est quidquid habet, est simplicissimum.

94. See Aquinas, *SCG* 1.22.10: "Now, names have been devised to signify the natures or essences of things. It remains, then, that the divine being is God's essence or nature" and *ST* 1.13.11 "Hence since the existence of God is his essence itself, which can be said of no other, it is clear that among other names this one specially denominates God."

95. See Davies, "A Modern Defence of Divine Simplicity," 558–59.

common sense notion that something does not *have* to exist.⁹⁶ An act of existing (*actus essendi*) for a created, contingent being is distinct from its essence, thereby making it composite; each created thing has its own act of existence that is ontologically distinct from itself. In this case, existence is understood as formal, or form-like, something that is conjoined to an individual thing; it is received into a thing and as such is a metaphysical part, parallel to its essence, accidents and matter (if it is a material substance).⁹⁷ To use modern terminology, existence functions as a first-level predicate and not as merely a second-level predicate.⁹⁸ Boethius explains, "Every simple being possesses as unity its being and its individual existence" (*De Hebd.* 45).⁹⁹ He means that for a simple being, in contrast to a composite being, it is *not* one thing to be what it is (*id quod est*) and another to exist (*esse*); in other words, its essence includes its existence. With respect to God no distinction can be made between essence and existence without making him into a composite: what God is to which is superadded God's existence. It is not one thing for God to be God and another thing for God to exist. Rather God's essence, what God is, cannot be distinguished from God's existence, his *actus essendi*, for otherwise God would consist of two parts. Likewise, Aquinas writes, "God is not only his own essence . . . but also his own existence (*ST* 1.3.4; see *SCG* 1.22.6).¹⁰⁰ Again to use modern terminology, what God is, or God's essence, is "necessarily self-instantiating."¹⁰¹

---

96. Patterson, *The Concept of God in the Philosophy of Aquinas*, 156–77; Hughes, *Complex Theory*, 3–59.

97. Ockham rejects the distinction between essence and existence, since to be existent signifies the thing itself, the essence; he does not, however, represent the majority view (*Summa totius logicae* III, II, c. xxvii). According to him, what is being expressed by saying that God is existence itself (*ipsum esse*) is God's necessity and independence.

98. As is often pointed out, for this assertion about God to be intelligible, existence must be considered a first-level predicate, an expression that generates a proposition when predicated of an individual. See Morreall, *Analogy and Talking about God: A Critique of the Thomistic Approach*, 69, 76; Williams, *What is Existence?*; Weigel, *Aquinas on Simplicity*, 57–90; 137–226.

99. Omne simplex esse suum et id quod est unum habet.

100. Deus non solum est sua essentia . . . sed etiam suum esse. See Patterson, *Concept of God*, 134–40; 194–209. Hughes concludes that Aquinas is missing a premise linking receiving existence and the property of being caused, i.e., he assumes that whatever participates in existence gets its existence from something else (*Complex Theory*, 51–54). Hughes's view is that God could still be considered as composite of essence and existence without contradiction, for otherwise God would only be his existence (55).

101. Burns, "The Status and Function of Divine Simpleness in *Summa Theologiae* Ia, qq. 2–13," 2.

The Oneness and Simplicity of God

Similarly, for Quenstedt the fifth type of composition from which God is exempt is that of *essentia et existentia*.[102] Because God is necessary, there is no difference between God's essence and his existence: God's essence is existence.[103] The assertion that God's essence is identical to his existence is known idiomatically as subsistent existence itself (*ipsum esse subsistens*).[104] When it is subsistent, being is an actual, individual thing, i.e., God, rather than just form-like, or a property.[105] Subsistent existence has for its opposite

102. Quenstedt, *Theologia didactico-polemica sive systema theologicum*, cap. VIII; sect. I, thesis XI; sect. II quaest. V.

103. Brian Davies's interpretation of subsistent existence ("that God and his existence are identical") is that "God owes his existence to nothing," and that God "is underived" ("The Doctrine of Divine Simplicity," 63).

104. Or *"ipsum esse per se subsistens"* (ST 1.4.2)

105. Aquinas's concept of subsistent existence is somewhat ambiguous (see Gilson, *Being and Some Philosophers*, 154–89; Kenny, *The Five Ways: St. Thomas Aquinas' Proofs of God's Existence*, 70–95; Kenny, *Aquinas*, 57–60). There are two possible meanings of Aquinas' assertion that God's essence is existence, a weaker and stronger one. The weaker meaning is that God is necessary because God's essence includes existence, whereas the stronger includes both the weaker meaning and the assertion that God has no essence other than existence. The stronger meaning is more pronounced in his earlier work *De ente et essentia*. Aquinas asserts that God has no essence or quiddity other than existence (5). Unlike all things, God is "being alone" (*esse tantum*) (5). Aquinas draws the further conclusion that God is not in a genus. Because God's essence is existence and existence is not a genus it follows that God is not in a genus. The reason that God cannot be other than existence is that to be so would make God composite. He explains, "But if we posit a thing that is existence only, such that it is subsisting existence itself, this existence will not receive the addition of a difference, for, if there were added a difference, there would be not only existence but existence and also beyond this some form" (4). Although he denies it, Aquinas' line of reasoning would seem to lead to the conclusion that, because his essence is existence, God is "that universal existence by which everything formally exists" (esse illud esse universale, quo quaelibet res formaliter est) (a synonym for universal existence is "common existence" [*esse commune*]) (5). In other words, it would seem to follow that to identify God's essence and existence implies that there are no limitations on God in the sense of ontological determination or contraction of being, which is at odds with any statement about the divine attributes. Aquinas, however, stops short of such a conclusion, claiming instead that the opposite is true. He explains, "But common existence, just as it does not include in its concept any addition, so too in its concept does it not exclude any addition" (5). He means that common existence does not exclude any addition that God by his goodness causes to be as other than himself so that created things are not simply manifestations of himself as existence. Moreover, Aquinas claims that to say that God is existence does not preclude attributing to him divine perfections, i.e., attributes or properties: "The remaining perfections and nobilities are not lacking in him" (5). This is because God has all the perfections that are found in every genus. Later in *Summa Theologiae*, Aquinas explains that indeed all perfections of things are in God in the sense of being caused by God as the first efficient cause (ST 1.4.2). First,

accidental and participated existence.[106] Of all the types of compositeness that are denied of God, this is the most controversial since it is thought to be an equivocation to call existence a predicate, insofar as, unlike other predicates, it adds nothing to the subject.

A sixth type of composition from which God is exempt, one that is often not included in such lists, is temporal composition. God's nature and existence cannot be divided into periods or phases, since God is eternal, being outside of time.[107] For God to consist of temporal parts would make him composite, in the same way as if he had physical or other metaphysi-

---

all perfections in things exist because of an efficient cause; a perfection in a thing as an effect pre-exists virtually in its efficient cause (effectus praeexistit virtute in causa agente). Moreover, as he explains, "To pre-exist virtually in the efficient cause is to pre-exist not in a more imperfect, but in a more perfect way." He means that the effect as it pre-exists in its cause exists more perfectly than its pre-existence in matter, which is to be acted upon by the efficient cause, insofar as matter is potentiality and therefore imperfect. (To exist virtually is to exist as contained or pre-existing in an efficient cause.) Therefore he concludes, "The perfections of all things must pre-exist in God in a more eminent way." (To exist eminently is to exist to a greater degree than something else of the same nature.) Second, if God is existence itself, then "God must contain within himself the perfection of being." In other words, Aquinas argues that an implication of the fact that God's essence is existence is that God is the cause of all existence. This means that the perfection of all things is caused by God. It should be noted, however, that the three quotations from Pseudo-Dionysius that Aquinas includes in support of his view do not really support his interpretation of how the perfections of all things are in God : "It is not that he is this and not that, but that he is all, as the cause of all"; "God exists not in any single mode, but embraces all being within himself, absolutely, without limitation, uniformly"; and "He is the very existence to subsisting things" (*De div. nom.* 5). Rather these are more consistent with a neoplatonic or even a panentheistic view.

106. Hughes argues that subsistent existence, the assertion that God is his own being, is not only unusual but unsupportable. To say that God is his existence is to assert the existence of existence, as if God could have only the one property of existence (*Complex Theory*, 3–59). He writes, "But it seems clear that nothing subsistent could be just existent: a mere existent substance is too thin to be possible" (21; see 57). He likewise rejects the corollary to the doctrine of subsistent existence, that all of God's attribute are identical with one another and with existence. Aquinas apparently thinks that having existence according to its full power, as God does, somehow entails having every perfection. Hughes questions, however, whether, unlike other properties, existence can be considered as having degrees: "By contrast there does not seem to be a difference between being perfectly existent and being less than perfectly existent. Existence is an on/off property: either you're there or you're not. Because existence is on/off, it would seem, either you have it according to its full power or you don't have it at all" (27) (see Miller, *A Most Unlikely God*, 15–26; 27–45).

107. Stump and Kretzmann, "Absolute Simplicity," 354; Morris, *Our Idea of God*, 114; Hoffman and Rosenkrantz, *The Divine Attributes*, 59–68.

The Oneness and Simplicity of God

cal parts. According to Aquinas, what characterizes God's eternity, which follows from God's simplicity and immutability, is being unending and instantaneous (*ST* 1.10.1). The result is that God cannot have a history, even though in the Bible God is portrayed as interactive in the unfolding of human history, in particular that of the Israelites. Prompted by his consideration of the Holy Spirit as gift, Augustine makes the distinction between what can be said about God relatively (*est relative dici*), but not accidentally since God is incapable of change, and what is said according to the substance of God (*De Trin.* V.17). Whatever is said about God in time is said about God relatively, which is to say with respect to God's relation to a temporal thing, for which something begins to be true.[108] Likewise, Anselm explains that God can be said to be in no time and in every time (*Monol.* 22).

Two Unusual Implications

There are two unusual implications that follow from the simplicity doctrine.[109] First, since God is simple, what appears to be discrete divine attributes distinct from God as their suppositum are really not.[110] In other words, there can be no distinction between God and any one of God's properties or even between God and all of God's properties. This is known as property-deity identification: there are no true divine attributes or properties because God is identical to his attributes or properties. The result is that God can be said to be an attribute or property and convertibly an attribute or a property can be said to be God.[111] From earliest times, this counterintuitive view has been part of the Christian understanding of God, being expressed

---

108. Along the same lines, Augustine writes, "But in the case of what is eternal, without beginning and without end, in whatever tense the verb is put, whether in the past, or present, or future, there is no falsehood thereby implied. For although to that immutable and ineffable nature, there is no proper application of Was and Will be, but only Is: for that nature alone is in truth, because incapable of change" (*Io. ev. tr.* XCIX.5). He finds this view of God implied in the divine name "I am that I am" (Exod 3:14) (*Civ. Dei* 11.21; *Conf.* 11). See also Clement of Alexandria *Paed.*, 1.8.71; Gregory Nazianzus, *Or.* 45.3.

109. See Dolezal, *God without Parts*, 125–63.

110. Mascall uses the illustration of different aspects of a building (*He Who Is: A Study in Traditional Theism*, 116–25). Just as a building will appear differently depending on the vantage point of the viewer, so God appears to have different attributes depending on limited human experience of God. Of course, his illustration assumes that God as simple is comparable to a building.

111. Hughes, *Complex Theory*, 70; Leftow, "Is God an Abstract Object?"; Gale, *On the Nature and Existence of God*, 23–29.

From God as Numerically One to God as Simple

using different terminology. Augustine argues at length that there is no distinction between God's substance and God's qualities (or what God begets) because this would introduce plurality into the substance of God (*Civ. Dei* XI.10). He writes, "Those things that are essentially and truly divine are called simple, because in them quality and substance are not distinct, nor do they participate in any deity, wisdom or beatitude" (XI.10.3).[112] Because God is simple, God's qualities are really one and the same with the divine substance: "And in him it is not one thing to be blessed, and another to be great, or wise, or true, or good, or indeed to be himself" (*De Trin.* VI.8; see XV.22). Rather, each quality predicated of God is wholly and necessarily God.[113] Along the same lines, because of God's simplicity Boethius concludes that Aristotle's ten categories do not apply to God, in particular the category of quality.[114] Rather than a substance, Boethius prefers to call God a substance that is beyond substance (*ultra substantia*) (*Trin.* 4).[115] Unlike a substance, it is the case both that God has no accidents and that the substantial or essential qualities are not separable from God. In other words, it is not one thing for God to be and another thing for God to be just, for example: "With him to be just and to be God are one and the same" (*Trin.* 4).[116] Similarly, influenced by Augustine, Lombard writes, "Moreover

112. Dicuntur illa simplicia, quae principaliter uereque divina sunt, quod non aliud est in eis qualitas, aliud substantia, nec aliorum participatione vel divina vel sapientia vel beata sunt.

113. See O'Meara, *Understanding Augustine*; Clark, "De Trinitate." In Book VII of *De Trinitate*, Augustine reconsiders the term substance (*substantia*) as applied to the Trinity and rejects it in favor of essence (*essentia*). This is because to subsist (*subsistare*), or to be a substance, is to admit of plurality, for a distinction is made between the substance and its attributes. Since God is simple, it is inappropriate to call God a substance or subject. He explains, "If, I say, God subsists so that he can be properly called a substance, then there is something in him as it were in a subject, and he is not simple, i.e., such that to him to be is the same as is anything else that is said concerning him in respect to himself; as, for instance, great, omnipotent, good, and whatever of this kind is not unfitly said of God. But it is an impiety to say that God subsists, and is a subject in relation to his own goodness, and that this goodness is not a substance or rather essence, and that God himself is not his own goodness, but that it is in him as in a subject. And hence it is clear that God is improperly called substance, in order that he may be understood to be, by the more usual name essence, which he is truly and properly called" (VII.5).

114. Mann, "Divine Simplicity," 454–55.

115. Marenbon, *Boethius*, 66–95.

116. Aquinas similarly concludes that, because he is being itself (*ens per se*), God cannot be considered to be a substance (*substantia*), by which is meant something that has a quiddity in it as a subject (*SCG* 1.25.10). The reason is that God has no quiddity is because being is not a genus. (Whatever has quiddity is in a genus, since quiddity is a

49

of this essence there is so great a simplicity and sincerity, that there is not in it anything that is not itself; but the same is the one having and what is had" (*Sent.* I. 8.8).[117] Finally, in the modern period the neo-orthodox theologian Karl Barth gives expression in his distinctive manner to this aspect of the simplicity doctrine.[118] He writes, "The multiplicity, individuality, and diversity of the divine perfections are those of the one divine being and therefore not those of another divine nature allied to it" (*CD* 2/1:331). His intention is to deny that the divine attributes add anything to God, as if God were composed of God-parts: "He does not possess this wealth. He is this wealth" (*CD* 2/1:331).[119] Barth holds that God's unity, freedom, and uniqueness are derivative of his simplicity. Functionally, for God to be a unity means that "in all that He is and does, He is wholly and undividedly Himself. At no time or place, then, is He divided or divisible" (*CD* 2/1:445). Barth connects God's simplicity with God's freedom insofar as, if he were influenced by a part of himself, then God would subordinated to it and not free. Finally, Barth affirms that God is unique because "within the Godhead there is no additional or subsequent being" (*CD* 2/1:45).[120]

The second unusual implication of the simplicity doctrine is that each of God's attributes is the same as all the others, so that each attribute denotes every other attribute, what is known as property-property identity. Schleiermacher defines divine simplicity as "the unseparated and inseparable mutual inherence of all divine attributes and activities," which means that each apparently discrete attribute or activity actually is the same as all of the other attributes and activities (*CF* 1 56.1). Human beings, however, incorrectly understand God's attributes and activities as a plurality, distinct from one another and from God himself as their suppositum. As implausible and

---

species and a species is determined to its genus.)

117. Huius autem essentiae simplicitas ac sinceritas tanta est, quod non est in ea aliquid, quod non sit ipsa; sed idem est habens et quod habetur.

118. *CD* 2/1:322–50; 440–90.

119. Franks, "The Simplicity of the Living God: Aquinas, Barth, and Some Philosophers," 293–97.

120. Karl Barth claims wrongly that the simplicity doctrine arose amidst attempts to clarify Trinitarian and Christological questions. Later theologians, especially Protestant ones, are said to have interpreted simplicity as a purely logical and metaphysical topic: "They give the impression that what is argued and considered is the general idea of a *ens vere unum* and not the God of the doctrine of the Trinity and of Christology" (*CD* 2/1:447). In fact, the simplicity doctrine made its way into Christian theology through Greek philosophy, which many early Christian theologians accepted unquestioningly. It was assumed that by definition God could be nothing but simple.

incoherent as it sounds, each attribute or property predicated of God is actually wholly and necessarily God and the same as all the other attributes or properties; this conclusion is viewed as an inescapable inference from the premise that God is simple.[121] To use modern terminology, by the transitivity of identity each attribute or property is identical with each of the others insofar as God is each of his attributes or properties. Augustine, whose works are quoted by many successive theologians, explains, "It is one and the same thing, therefore, to call God eternal, or immortal, or incorruptible, or unchangeable; and it is likewise one and the same thing to say that he is living, and that he is intelligent, that is, in truth, wise" (*De Trin.* XV.7). Similarly, Anselm draws the conclusion that each ostensive part of God is really the whole and that each part is the same as every other part: "Therefore, since this nature is in no respect composite and yet is in every respect those very many goods, all those goods must be one rather than many. Hence, each one of them is the same as all [the others]—whether they be considered distinctly or all together" (*Monol.* 17). In his view, a true understanding of God precludes all plurality: "Therefore life and wisdom and your other attributes are not parts of you but are all one, and every one of them is wholly what you are and what the other attributes are" (*Prosl.* 18). Protestant theologians likewise adopt the view of the mutual identity of the divine attributes or properties and their identity with God. John Owen explains, "*The attributes of God, which alone seem to be distinct things in the essence of God, are all of them essentially the same as one another, and every one the same with the essence of God itself*" (*Vind.* XII.72).[122] Even Barth embraces the property-property identity implication of the simplicity doctrine: "Our doctrine therefore means that every individual perfection in God is nothing but God Himself and therefore nothing but every other divine perfection" (*CD* 2/1:333).[123] So

---

121. Gregory of Nyssa argues that all the divine attributes are interconnected and interdependent (*Or. Cat.* 20).

122. See Gerhard, *Loci theologici*, locus secundus, caput viii, sect. iii; Quenstedt, *Theologia didactico-polemica sive systema theologicum*, cap. VIII; sect. II, quaest. II.

123. Barth adds, "It means equally strictly on the other hand that God Himself is nothing other than each one of His perfections in its individuality, and that each individual perfection is identical with every other and with the fullness of them all" (*CD* 2/1:333). He distinguishes his view from the semi-nominalistic interpretation, according to which God's simplicity has interpretive priority over God's multiplicity: "that in the last resort we can speak of the *proprietates Dei* only *improprie*, that the most characteristic inner being of God is a *simplicitas* which is to be understood undialectically" (*CD* 2/1:333; see *CD* 2/1:446–47). Barth warns that divine simplicity should not be so theologically dominant that it becomes "an idol, which, devouring everything concrete,

The Oneness and Simplicity of God

unusual is the conclusion of the mutual identification of God's attributes or properties that John Duns Scotus is led to reject it as theological nonsense; he modifies it with the goal of avoiding the formal identification of God's attributes or properties, what he calls God's perfections, with one another, which to him is impossible. He agrees that, unlike a finite composite, the infinite is self-identical, so that it is impossible for it to consist of different parts not identical to one another and each lacking the perfection of the whole.[124] He takes exception to the view, however, that this implies that God's attributes or properties are formally identical.[125] Duns Scotus is, however, a rare dissenting voice to the consensus.

---

stands behind all these formulae" (*CD* 2/1:329). His view bears the Hegelian influence of the concept of the true infinite.

124. Duns Scotus affirms that even though they are *really* identical, God's attributes or properties, what he calls God's perfections, are not *formally* identical to one another. The difference between God and created things with respect to the nature of predication is an implication of the former's infinity. Because each divine attribute is infinite with respect to its mode, it follows that God's attributes are numerically identical. This is because of the nature of infinity: since nothing can be added to infinity, it is impossible for infinite attributes to be combined to become a composite that is greater than each of its parts. In other words, infinite attributes cannot be parts of a composite. Duns Scotus concludes that, since infinite attributes do not and cannot co-exist as parts of a composite, each formally-distinct, infinite attribute contains in itself the idea of its identity with all other formally-distinct, infinite attributes. If one abstracted from a finite thing its attributes and consider each as separate from its suppositum and from the other attributes, the result would be that the attributes would lose the basis of their unity and identity with the other attributes. Since formally they are different from one another, there is no cause to assert that they have unity and identity in the absence of the suppositum to which the attributes belong. In the case of God, who is infinite, however, the opposite is true. Without losing its formal distinctiveness, each infinite divine attribute is really identical to the other attributes and to God as their possessor (*Ord.* 1.8.1.4, nn. 213, 219–20) (see Cross, *Duns Scotus on God*, 99–114). By contrast, Aquinas is content to live with the apparent contradiction that God's attributes are really one even though the limited human intellect cannot conceive God's unity except as a plurality. He writes, "God, however, as considered in himself, is altogether one and simple, yet our intellect knows him by different conceptions because it cannot see him as he is in himself. Nevertheless, although it understands him under different conceptions, it knows that one and the same simple object corresponds to its conceptions. Therefore the plurality of predicate and subject represents the plurality of idea; and the intellect represents the unity by composition" (*ST* 1.13.12).

125. Duns Scotus explains, "For infinity does not destroy the formal idea of that to which it is added, because in whatever grade some perfection is understood to be (which 'grade' however is a grade of that perfection), the formal idea of that perfection is not taken away because of that grade, and so if it as it is general does not include it formally as it is in general, neither does it as infinite include it formally as it is infinite" (Infinitas enim non destruit formalem rationem illius cui additur, quia in quocumque gradu intelligatur esse aliqua perfectio (qui tamen 'gradus' est gradus illius perfectionis), non

From God as Numerically One to God as Simple

Theologians have invented terminological distinctions to explain how God can be simple but still appear to have attributes or properties. John of Damascus claims that there is a difference between God's essence (οὐσία), which is simple, and his multiform nature (φύσις), expressible as God's attributes or properties.[126] He writes, "Again, goodness and justice and piety and such like names belong to the nature (τῇ φύσει), but do not explain his actual essence (οὐσίαν)" (*O.F.* 1.9). Similarly, Anselm explains that whatever God is essentially God is in one "mode" (*modus*) or "consideration" (*consideratio*), by which he means to deny that God has a plurality of attributes that collectively constitute God's essence (*Monol.* 17).[127] Exegeting Rom 1:20, Lombard makes a distinction between "the invisible things of God," by which is meant God's attributes appearing to human beings in "many modes" (*pluribus modis*), and God as "one and simple essence" (*una . . . et simplex essentia*) (*Sent.* I.3.1). Because their experience is multifaceted, human beings unavoidably but inaccurately understand God as having attributes. He explains, for example, that God's attribute of being the eternal founder is understood by the perpetuity of creatures, his attribute of omnipotence from the magnitude of creatures, his wisdom from their order and disposition and his goodness from his governance of them. Yet God remains one, not having many attributes. Likewise Aquinas distinguishes between the different conceptions (*diversas conceptiones*) under which the intellect understands the one and simple God, as God is in himself, the former being an accommodation (*ST* 1.13.12; see 1.2.3). Another strategy in dealing with the difficulties of the simplicity doctrine is to make a distinction between God and God's energies (ἐνέργειαι): what God does is not what God is. What can be known about God is God's energies, which describes God's modes of action and interaction with created beings.[128]

---

tollitur formalis ratio illius perfectionis propter istum gradum, et ita si non includit formaliter 'ut in communi, in communi', nec 'ut infinitum, infinitum') (*Ord.* 1.8.1.4, n. 192).

126. So positive attributes or properties, as opposed to negative ones that deny that God has some attribute, are expressions of God's nature and not his essence.

127. Anselm writes, "Whatever is predicated essentially of the supreme substance is one, so whatever the supreme substance is essentially it is in one way, in one respect (ita ipsa uno modo una consideration est, quidquid est essentialiter)" (*Monol.* 17).

128. Cyril of Alexandria also explains that God in himself is self-identical, always being the same: "being in all things like himself" (ἐν πᾶσιν ὅμοιος ὢν αὐτὸς ἑαυτῷ) (*Cat. lect.* 6.7). Along the same lines, Basil addresses the accusation that he inconsistently holds both that God is simple (ἁπλοῦς) and that many attributes or properties can be assigned to God, such as greatness, power, wisdom, goodness, providence, and the justness of his judgment (*Ep.* 234). He maintains his belief in the simplicity of God by distinguishing between

The Oneness and Simplicity of God

Cyril of Alexander writes, "For though he is called good, just, almighty and Sabaoth, he is not on that account diverse and various (διάφορος καὶ ἀλλοῖος); but being one and the same (εἷς ὢν καὶ ὁ αὐτός), he sends forth countless energies of his Godness (τὰς τῆς θεότητος ἐνεργείας)" (*Cat. lect.* 6.7). Cyril distinguishes between the one and same God and God's many energies, or operations, described by God's many names, or attributes. The latter functions as an inadequate substitute for the former. Aquinas offers a variation of this view. Because they have no knowledge of the divine essence, human beings can only know God through God's effects (*effectus*) (*SCG* 1.31; see *ST* 1.13.4). These attributes or perfections, which find partial, analogous expression in created things, are the effects of one and the same power (*virtus*), which is identified with God's simple essence and to God.[129] It is safe to say, however, that such theological devices for mitigating the counterintuitive nature of the simplicity doctrine are circular insofar as they presuppose that such a distinction needs to be made at all; for this reason they have only rhetorical value. This makes it all the more imperative that reasons for holding the simplicity doctrine be produced.

The doctrine of the Trinity complicates matters for Christian theologians who hold to the simplicity doctrine.[130] They must deny that the fact that God exists in three persons (*personae*) constitutes a type of composition in God, but at the same time avoiding the pitfall of Sabellianism or modalism, that the divine persons are only functions or aspects of the one God. Against Photinianism, for example, Johann Gerhard writes, "Now in

---

God's essence (οὐσία), which is simple, and his energies or operations (αἱ ἐνέργειαι), which are many. The difference between them is that essence is what God is, which is beyond human understanding, whereas energies are what God does, of which human beings have experience. He writes, "His energies come down to us, but his essence remains beyond our reach" (αἱ μὲν γὰρ ἐνέργειαι αὐτοῦ πρὸς ὑμᾶς καταβαίνουσιν, ἡ δὲ οὐσία αὐτοῦ μένει ἀπρόσιτος). He considers Eunomius's view that God's essence is to be ingenerate as naïve, insofar as he does not recognize a distinction between God's energies (αἱ ἐνέργειαι), what God does, the semantic equivalent of the divine attributes, and God's essence (*Ep.* 234.3). In Basil's view, God's attributes or properties singly or collectively cannot describe the essence of God because God is one and simple (see *Adv. Eunom.* II.29).

129. Aquinas writes, "So, too, the perfections of all things, which belong to the rest of things through diverse forms, must be attributed to God through one and the same power in him. This power is nothing other than his essence, since, as we have proved, there can be no accident in God" (Ita et omnium perfectiones, quae rebus aliis secundum diversas formas conveniunt, Deo secundum unam eius virtutem attribui est necesse. Quae item virtus non est aliud a sua essentia: cum ei nihil accidere possit, ut probatum est) (*SCG* 1.31).

130. In treatments of God's simplicity there is usually included a section in which it is explained how the three divine persons are not an indication of compositeness.

From God as Numerically One to God as Simple

truth three divine persons are one and indivisible essence."[131] Generally, Christian theologians assert that being triune is not a real type of composition. In fact, as already explained, the simplicity doctrine allows Christian theologians to distinguish between the three divine persons without denying unity of God.[132] To say that the confession of God as Father, Son and Holy Spirit does not compromise divine unity and simplicity, however, appears to be bare assertion, and could justifiably be labeled by critics as question-begging, perhaps concealing a type of neo-Sabellianism.

---

131. Jam vero trium divinarum personarum est una atque indivisa essentia (Gerhard, *Loci Theologici*, locus secundus, caput viii, sect. III §134). As explained by Gregory of Nyssa, Eunomius argues that Gregory and his orthodox allies, contrary to their own claims, view God as composite (σύνθετος) because, while asserting that the Father and Son are both light, they nevertheless separate "the one Light from the other by certain special attributes and various differences (ἰδιότησι δέ τισι καὶ ποικίλιας διαφοραῖς)" (*Con. Eunom.* 3.10.46). The claim is that, if God is incomposite and the Son is supposed to have the same essence as the Father, there can be no differences between the Father and the Son. Gregory's response is to differentiate between the divine essence (οὐσία) and "community and specific difference" (κοινότης τε καὶ ἰδιότης), by which is meant the differences between the Father and the Son, who nonetheless have the same essence or divine nature (*Con. Eunom.* 3.10.48).

132. Bernard Lonergan argues for the orthodox position that "the divine essence and the real divine relation are really the same" (*The Triune God: Systematics*, 259). In his view, there are three possibilities for how divinity and paternity could relate to each other: they are either really different and not a composite, really different and a composite or really the same. By a process of elimination Lonergan reaches the conclusion that the third option is the only theologically viable one. If divinity and paternity are really different and not composite, then the Father is not God, which is obviously heretical. If divinity and paternity are really different and composite then God is not simple, which is equally unacceptable. He writes, "If we choose the second, God is not simple, there is a cause of God's composition, and therefore God is not the first principle, which is likewise heretical." This leaves only the third option, that divinity and paternity are really the same. In other words, God the Father is his divine essence or nature; the same also applies to the God the Son and God the Holy Spirit. The possibility of conceiving of divinity as something that is added to each of the persons of the Trinity thereby making a quarternity and not a trinity is excluded. What is of interest is that Lonergan can assume divine simplicity as a premise from which to draw conclusions about the nature of the Triune God. He does not consider the question of whether God should be considered simple as problematic in any way.

3

Traditional Argumentation for the Simplicity Doctrine

IN ADDITION TO THE appeal to tradition, Christian theologians proffer two types of arguments for the simplicity doctrine. First, scriptural support is adduced, an approach that tends to be favored by Protestant theologians because of their commitment to grounding all theological assertion in Scripture. Second, from a consideration of the nature of God, arguments often assuming an Aristotelian ontology are put forward in order to prove that God can be nothing but simple.[1] Neither type of argument, however, is persuasive.

Scriptural Proofs for God's Simplicity

There is nothing directly stated in Scripture that would lead one to think of God as simple or incomposite. The question of whether God has component parts of whatever type is never entertained. Since it never explicitly says so, theologians look for statements in Scripture from which God's simplicity can be inferred. First, some hold that God's simplicity is implied in the biblical assertions that God is numerically one, such as Deut 4:35 "YHWH, he is God; there is no other besides him and Deut 6:4 "Hear, O Israel. YHWH is our God, YHWH is one."[2] It is assumed that to be numeri-

---

1. See Zanchi, *De Natura Dei, De Attributis*, lib. 2, cap. 2.

2. For example, Quenstedt, *Theologia didactico-polemica sive systema theologicum*, caput VIII; sect. II, quaestia V; Turretin, *Institutio Theologiae Elencticae*, locus tertius,

cally one and to be simple are convertible, so that if God is one of them then God necessarily is the other. To use traditional theological terminology, if he is asserted to be *unitas singularitatis*, God must also be *unitas simplicitatis*. Athanasius, for instance, takes for granted that the confession of the one God in the Bible means the one *and simple* God (*De syn.* 35).[3] Likewise, Basil explains that God is one precisely because God is simple: "God alone is called a monad and one because it is God's nature to be simple, which makes him incomprehensible" (*Ep.* 8).[4] Aquinas assumes that oneness in the biblical sense of numerical oneness is convertible with simplicity, being the negation of division. To call God one is say that God is simple, which means that God is undivided both actually and potentially (*ST* 1.11.4). For this reason he argues for the maximal oneness of God from the simplicity of God: "But he [God] is maximally undivided (*maxime indivisum*) inasmuch as he is divided neither actually nor potentially, by any mode of division; since he is altogether simple, as was shown above. Hence it is manifest that God is maximally one (*maxime unus*)." Similarly, Italian Reformer Girolamo Zanchi claims that, contrary to the one who would protest that it is an unnecessary doctrine, the simplicity of God guarantees the oneness of the triune God.[5] Finally, Swiss Reformed theologian Francis Turretin collapses the two different types of oneness into one: "Who is absolutely one is indeed absolutely simple, and who for that reason therefore is unable to be divided or composite."[6] No argument, however, is provided for why being numerically one is necessarily correlated with being one in the sense of being simple or incomposite, even though clearly these are two different types of oneness. It is safe to say that the movement from God as numerically one to God as simple is suppositional and without justification.

---

quaest. VII.IV. See Heidegger, *Corpus theologiae christianae*, locus tertius, xxxii; Bavinck, *Reformed Dogmatics*, vol. 2, *God and Creation*, 173–77.

3. Athanasius writes, "But if, when we hear it said, 'I am that I am,' and, 'In the beginning God created the heaven and the earth,' and, 'Hear, O Israel, the Lord our God is one Lord,' and, 'Thus says the Lord Almighty', we understand nothing else than the very simple, and blessed, and incomprehensible essence itself of him that is (οὐχ ἕτερόν τι ἀλλ' αὐτὴν τὴν ἁπλῆν καὶ μακααρίαν καὶ ἀκατάκηπτον τοῦ ὄντος οὐσίαν νοοῦμεν)."

4. ἡ δὲ μονὰς καὶ ἑνὰς τῆς ἁπλῆς καὶ ἀπεριλήπτου οὐσίας ἐστι' σημαντική.

5. Zanchi, *De Natura Dei, De Attributis*, lib. 2, cap. 2. He writes, "Deinde ex ista simplicatate, sequitor confirmatio doctrinae de uno duntaxat Deo, licet tres sint personae."

6. Qui est absolute unus, est etiam absolute simplex, quique ideo divide nequit, vel componi (*Institutio Theologiae Elencticae* I, loc. tertius, quaest. VII.IV).

The Oneness and Simplicity of God

Second, the fact that John 4:24 asserts that "God is spirit" is said to imply that God is simple. On the assumption that the divine attributes of being infinite, simple, and spiritual are convertible, Puritan theologian Stephen Charnock argues that if God is a spirit, as John 4:24 indicates, then God is necessarily infinite and simple: "If there were such a division of his being, he would not be the most simple and uncompounded being, but would be made up of various parts; he would not be a Spirit."[7] Zanchi also assumes that to be a spirit is to be simple by nature, in contrast to a corporeal being, and God as *uncreated* spirit must be most simple. To be such would exclude all composition, not just the corporeal type.[8] The conclusion that God as spirit is convertible with simplicity, however, assumes that human beings know what it means for God to be spirit, that being spirit is not simply a theological negation: God is *not* physical. Moreover, the alleged convertibility of being spirit and being simple is nothing more than bare assertion, since no evidence is provided for it. It is not at all obvious that to be spirit is to be simple, especially since there is nothing contradictory about conceiving spirits as having metaphysical parts, as created spirits such as angels are thought to have. Nineteenth-century Protestant theologian Charles Hodge likewise infers the simplicity of God from the fact that, as stated in the Westminster Catechism (Q. 7), John 4:24 affirms that God is a spirit. Presupposing a univocity between God as spirit and created spirits, he argues that, since created spirits are simple, how much more must God be simple.[9] He writes, "Whatever is essential to the idea of a spirit, as learned from our own consciousness, is to be referred to God as determining his nature."[10] Because they know intuitively that their souls are one and simple, human beings know by inference God's unity and simplicity.[11] It is debatable, however, whether one can assume that what is true of

---

7. Charnock, *The Complete Works of Stephen Charnock*, vol. 1, *Discourses on Divine Providence and The Existence and Attributes of God*, 430. Charnock takes it as axiomatic that to be infinite is to be simple: "Whatsoever hath parts is finite, but God is infinite, therefore hath no parts of his essence" (430).

8. Zanchi, *De Natura Dei, De Attributis*, lib. 2, cap. 2. This verse is sometimes paired with thematically-related Exod 3:14–15. Similarly, Gerhard without argumentation asserts that for God to be a "spiritual essence" (Exod 3:14) or "spirit" (John 4:24) signifies "an infinite thing (res), one in number, actually existing, utterly simple" (*Loci theologici*, locus secundus, caput vi §95).

9. See Novatian, *De Trin.* 5; Didymus of Alexandria, *De spir. sancto* 35; Heidegger, *Corpus theologiae christianae*, locus tertius, xxxii; Aquinas, ST 1.3.4, 7.

10. Hodge, *Systematic Theology*, 1.377.

11. Ibid., 1.378.

Traditional Argumentation for the Simplicity Doctrine

created spirits is true of God as spirit, that there is a univocity between the two. In addition, to claim to know intuitively that created spirits are simple is open to question.[12] The nature of the non-corporeal aspect of a human being, known variously as spirit or soul, is difficult to know, not being open to direct inspection. To assume that anything that is incorporeal is by definition simple is ill-advised. What is required is a rationalistic argument to the effect that spirits or minds, as opposed to bodies, are known analytically to be simple, but such an argument would probably not be convincing to an empiricist or critical philosopher.[13]

Third, God's self-revelation in Exod 3:14 "I am who I am"[14] and its putative parallel in Rev 1:4 "who was, is and is to come" is interpreted as implying God's simplicity. John of Damascus holds that, because of God's simplicity, the most appropriate name for God is "the one who is" (ὁ ὤν) (Exod 3:14) (O.F. 9). According to him, God is not a composite, but is simple, which means that God has no true attributes or properties. This is why Exod 3:14 refers to God by the tautologous appellation "I am the one who is." The reason that God has a name that is not really a name is that, insofar as he is simple, nothing can be predicated of God, not even his essence or nature. Rather to say that God is "the one who is" means that "he comprehending in himself the whole has being like a sea of essence infinite and unseen," which seems to mean *inter alia* that God is all things and therefore no particular thing that can be identified by a predicate.[15] Along similar exegetical lines, it is argued that YHWH identifies himself tautologously as "I am what I am" in Exod 3:14 because he is both his own being and his own essence, from which it follows that he cannot but be simple. Zanchi claims that the divine name Iohoua (YHWH), which is translated as "he is" (*Est*) with no predicate completion, means that God derives his being and essence from himself and not from another (thereby making God first).[16] The point is that God is not distinct from his essence or existence, from which it follows that God must be simple.[17] Likewise, Lutheran scholastic

12. As Kant explains in his *Critique of Pure Reason* (A351–61).

13. Along Thomistic lines, Garrigou-Lagrange assumes that whatever is simple must be spirit (*God, His Existence and Nature*, vol. 2, *A Thomistic Solution to Certain Agnostic Antinomies*, 17).

14. LXX ἐγώ εἰμι ὁ ὤν: "I am the one who is."

15. ὅλον γὰρ ἐν ἑαυτῷ συλλαβὼν ἔχει τὸ εἶναι, οἷον τι πέλαγος οὐσίας ἄπειρον καὶ ἀόριστον.

16. Zanchi, *De Natura Dei, De Attributis*, lib. 2, cap. 2.

17. In his exposition of John 4:24 "God is spirit," Charnock asserts that the divine

theologian Johannes Quenstedt holds that God is simple because, as Exod 3:14 asserts, God is his being and because God is his own essence. The implication is that this can be true only of a simple being. He also argues *a parte rei* from the identification of God in Rev 1:4 as "the one who is, was and will be" to God's complete simplicity. If God has no temporal divisions but rather simultaneity (*non divisum, sed conjunctum et simul*), then it follows that God is simple in all respects.[18] However, even if it is legitimate to interpret God's self-revelation in Exod 3:14 as a disclosure of God's unique mode of being, it is still an exegetical leap from that to God as simple. It is questionable whether so much theological content can be extracted from Exod 3:14. Based on Exod 3:14 the most that could be said is that God is his own being or being-itself in the sense of being ingenerate and necessary.

Fourth, the fact that in Scripture God is sometimes is identified with abstract nouns, such as light (John 1:4, 5) and love (1 John 4:16), rather than being described by means of the corresponding adjectives, is said to imply that God is simple.[19] This is because God can only be described in this manner if God is his own essence, rather than being a suppositum that has certain essential attributes expressed as adjectival subjective completions; for God to be God's own essence means that God is simple. As Aquinas explains, "And as God is simple, and subsisting, we attribute to him abstract names to signify his simplicity" (*ST* 1.13.1).[20] Herman Bavinck also finds this argument for the simplicity doctrine convincing: "Scripture to denote the fullness of the life of God, uses not only adjectives but also substantives."[21] It is more likely, however, that identifying God with one of his attributes or properties is a literary device designed to express that God truly or supremely is characterized by the attribute or property named. It is unadvisable to place too much theological weight on this literary usage.

---

name "I am that I am" means "a simple, pure, uncompounded being, without any created mixture" (*The Complete Works of Stephen Charnock*, vol. 1, *Discourses on Divine Providence and The Existence and Attributes of God*, 264). In his view, this proves that God is spiritual and incorporeal.

18. Quenstedt, *Theologia didactico-polemica sive systema theologicum*, caput VIII, sect. II, quaestia V polemica. See Polanus, *Syntagma theologiae christianae*, lib. 2, caput IIX; Heidegger, *Corpus theologiae christianae*, locus tertius, xxxii.

19. Zanchi, *De Natura Dei, De Attributis*, lib. 2. cap. 2; Gerhard, *Loci theologici*, locus secundus, caput viii, sect. III §129; Quenstedt, *Theologia didactico-polemica sive systema theologicum*, caput VIII, sect. II, quaest. V; Heidegger, *Corpus theologiae christianae*, locus tertius, xxxii). Bavinck, *Reformed Dogmatics*, vol. 2, *God and Creation*, 173–77.

20. Quia igitur et Deus simplex est, et subsistens est, attribuimus ei et nomina abstracta.

21. Bavinck, *Reformed Dogmatics*, vol. 2, *God and Creation*, 173.

Traditional Argumentation for the Simplicity Doctrine

The arguments from Scripture for God's simplicity are weak to the point of being unconvincing; that God is simple or incomposite is neither stated directly in Scripture nor even implied.[22] The fact that the simplicity doctrine has its origin in Greek philosophy explains why the arguments advanced from Scripture tend to be forced and tenuous: it appears as a *corpus alienum* in the biblical portrayal of God.[23] For this reason, in spite of their now-sullied reputation, the Remonstrants were correct that the simplicity doctrine was not scriptural but what they referred to as "metaphysical."[24] Nevertheless, not being biblical in origin does not necessarily mean that the simplicity doctrine is mistaken. It is only to say that, if it is to be accepted, it is requisite that the doctrine be shown to be a valid inference from the nature of God, a necessary corollary of other of God's attributes or properties that are explicit in Scripture.

Proofs for God's Simplicity from the Nature of God

Theologians have argued that the nature of God is such that God cannot be other than simple: to conceive God as composite in any respect is logically contradictory. The theological methodology used is analytical insofar as divine simplicity is explicative of the concept of God. In other words, to affirm that God is simple is a deduction of an implied proposition about God from an explicit proposition. In some cases there is overlap in these arguments because the divine attributes or properties sometimes are not completely conceptually distinct from one another.[25] Some of these arguments are found in non-Christian and even pre-Christian sources, a fact that probably indicates a borrowing by Christian theologians. These proofs for the simplicity doctrine are unconvincing for one reason or another.

It is important to recognize the role that presuppositions play in arguments for the simplicity doctrine from the nature of God.[26] Some of

---

22. Feinberg, *No One Like Him*, 327–29.

23. Ibid., 327–29. Edward Wierenga declines to discuss the simplicity doctrine because of its origin in Greek philosophy (*The Nature of God*, 173).

24. See Turretin, *Institutio Theologiae Elencticae*, locus tertius, quaest. VII.I.

25. On this topic, see Dolezal, *God without Parts*, 67–92; Hughes, *Complex Theory*, 1–148.

26. A few of the arguments for simplicity based on the nature of God are unconvincing even granting the presuppositions of the respective argument, for which reason these can be set aside.

The Oneness and Simplicity of God

the arguments advanced have Greek philosophical presuppositions. Of particular importance is the presupposition that simplicity is ontologically superior to compositeness, which is so foundational and pervasive that no one sees the need to argue for its validity. In some cases, the arguments are more narrowly dependent upon Aristotelian substance metaphysics with its philosophical categories of gradations of being, matter and form, potentiality and actuality, efficient causation, as well as genus and species (differentia).[27] Such arguments are not usually convincing to theologians who do not share these presuppositions. To the theologian who methodologically takes a skeptical stance towards all philosophy, eschewing any prior ideological commitment, such arguments can even be judged to be meaningless. Often the arguments for God's simplicity put forward have common-sense presuppositions based on universal human experience of the physical world. The axioms that the parts of a physical composite are temporally and ontologically prior to the whole of which they are parts, that a pre-existing cause is required for physical parts to coalesce into a whole, and that a physical composite is liable to decomposition arguably would have few detractors. Even on these common-sense presuppositions, however, the arguments for the simplicity doctrine still fall short of proof.

Most arguments for the simplicity doctrine, including the more common-sense type of arguments, depend upon two basic, often-unstated presuppositions, both of which are open to question. First it is presupposed that a metaphysical part is a unitive concept, signifying one type of thing.

---

27. Karl Barth rejects the usual philosophical foundation of God simplicity, claiming that such an approach objectifies the concept of simplicity and then names it God. In other words, on the traditional understanding the assertion of the simplicity of God is reversible: the simple is God and God is the simple. Alluding to Feuerbach's critique of religion, he claims that the simple God is a projection and deification of the human longing to be less complex (*CD* II/1 449). Such is a "very natural object of human divining and construction" (*CD* II/1 449). Instead Barth argues that the doctrine of God's simplicity, "this incomparable and undivided being" (*CD* II/1 450), can be inferred from God's acts. God's simplicity is known from the incomparability and therefore uniqueness of God self-revelation, "the encounter between man and God, brought about by God" (*CD* II/1 450). He adds, "It is in His love above all that God reveals Himself as the One who is incomparable and therefore unique" (*CD* II/1 450). In particular, it is in God's election, "a choice as an event" (*CD* II/1 451), in which God's uniqueness and therefore simplicity is revealed. He writes, "It is in this event as such that the love of God reveals itself and acts with the incomparability to which the only appropriate response is the confession of God's uniqueness" (*CD* II/1 451). Barth's derivation of the simplicity doctrine from God's self-revelation is not even remotely convincing. At most from God's incomparable acts one could infer that God is greater in power than any other causal agent, but not that God is simple. Barth would be better to abandon the doctrine as ungroundable in God's freedom in love.

This explains, for example, why the second-level predicate of existence can be included as a metaphysical part along with first-level predicates, such as omniscience or omnipotence. The possibility that what are considered metaphysical parts are only superficially so, having in common merely the fact that grammatically they are predicates, is not contemplated. Second, it is assumed that metaphysical types of compositeness are to be understood on analogy with physical compositeness.[28] It is presupposed that both physical and metaphysical types of compositeness are the same thing in spite of the obvious differences. The fact that in ordinary language the term "part" has different types of reference is taken to mean that being composite is genus-like. Both physical and metaphysical types of compositeness are understood to be generically identical, so that by virtue of having either type of part a thing can be said to be composite. It is further presupposed that, because a so-called metaphysical part is generically identical to a physical part, such as a bodily part, what is true of latter *mutatis mutandis* is also true of the former. The possibility is usually not entertained, however, that ordinary language may be misleading insofar as a metaphysical part may only be "part" in a borrowed, metaphorical sense. In other words, the possibility that term "part" may be polyvalent and therefore its use may be equivocal is not considered. Such a position would preclude the possibility of extrapolating from the nature of the better-known physical part to a determination of the nature of the lesser-known metaphysical part.

From God as First

God's simplicity is said to follow from the fact that God is the first of all things; as such, God is uncaused and ontologically independent. To be first implies having aseity, which, to use modern philosophical terminology, means that God has an asymmetrical dependence-relation to created things.[29] In his *Summa Theologiae*, Aquinas, for example, places simplicity at the head of a list of divine attributes that follow from God as first cause

---

28. Few theologians hold that God has or is body, with quantitatively distinct physical parts. Usually the denial that God is physically composite is perfunctory and serves as a preamble to the further denial that God is metaphysically composite.

29. Brower, "Simplicity and Aseity," 106–8; Bavinck, *Reformed Dogmatics*, vol. 2, *God and Creation*, 152; Plantinga, *Does God Have a Nature?*, 28–35; Dolezal, *God without Parts*, 68–72. Simplicity is included as an expression of God's aseity. To be *a se* and not *ab alio* is to be from oneself in the sense of being independent of all things for one's existence.

(*ST* 1.1.3). There are three variations of the argument for divine simplicity from God as first.

In the first variation it is argued that, if God were composite in any sense, then God's parts would be ontologically prior to God, who would consist of these parts.[30] It follows that God would not be first, but would be ontologically posterior to his parts and so would lack what has been called mereological priority.[31] For this reason God would no longer have aesity, but rather be dependent on his parts for his essence and existence. For God to be conceived as such is a contradiction because God is absolutely first. Origen writes, "But God, who is the principle (*principium*) of all things, is not to be regarded as a composite being (*compositum*), in case perhaps there should be found to exist elements prior to the principle itself, out of which everything is composed, whatever that be which is called composite" (*Prin.* 1.6). The principle of all things is the first cause of all things; it follows that this principle can have no pre-existing parts. Along the same lines, Aquinas explains, "Every composite is posterior to its component parts, and is dependent on them, but God is the first being" (*ST* 1.3.7).[32] He holds that, if God were composed of physical or metaphysical parts, it would follow that God would be composed of what is not God, since a part is not the whole; this would be contradictory for God the first being, since he would no longer be first, but subsequent to his parts.[33] Aquinas adds that it is contradictory to say that God, the first being who is before all things, is a multitude since multitudes are posterior to and depend upon unities, by which is meant self-identical parts (*SCG* 1.18). He writes, "Again, prior to all multitude we must find unity. But there is multitude in every composite. Therefore, that which is before all things, namely, God, must be free of all composition" (*SCG* 1.18.8). Introducing a distinctly Aristotelian concept, Aquinas also claims that, since he is form itself (*ipsa forma*), God is what he is, because "in the form itself, there is nothing besides itself." But a part of a composite cannot be said to be the whole: "Nothing composite can be predicated of any single one of its parts" (*ST* 1.3.7).[34] What is said about a

30. Holmes, "'Something Much Too Plain to Say': Towards a Defense of the Doctrine of Divine Simplicity," 150–53.

31. Hughes, *Complex Theory*, 33. He also uses the term "one-way ontological dependence" (30).

32. Omne compositum est posterius suis componentibus, et dependens ex eis. Deus autem est primum ens. See *SCG* 1.18.3; *Sent.* 8.4).

33. See Hughes, *Complex Theory*, 33–50.

34. See Holloway, *An Introduction to Natural Theology*, 232–34; Weigel, *Aquinas on*

part is not true of the composite of which it is a part and vice versa. Thus, it is clear that God as form itself cannot be composite, for otherwise God as the whole would be something besides himself, namely his parts. The fact that God is form itself implies his simplicity, that he could not be his parts, since each part and even all the parts would not be the whole.

The first variation of the argument from God as first to divine simplicity can be shorn of its Aristotelian elements: the argument that God is simple because God is form itself (*ipsa forma*) is not meaningful to anyone who is not an Aristotelian. What remains is an argument that is an extrapolation from the common-sense axiom that the parts of a physical composite are prior to the whole of which they are parts. This axiom is generalized to apply to God, who has only metaphysical parts, since God has or is no body. Because God is first, God's accidents, essential attributes, and even his existence could not be parts of God because they would be ontologically, though not temporarily, prior to him. Two problems with this argument can be raised. First it can be questioned whether the concept of a metaphysical part is nothing more than a metaphor. If so, then an extrapolation from the nature of physical parts to that of so-called metaphysical parts is disallowed. It would seem that the term "part" is being used equivocally when such diverse things as existence and a bodily part can be considered as "parts" of a thing. Second, even if thinking about God in terms of metaphysical parts is valid, Hughes plausibly argues that God as first could still be composite as long as the parts were not things that could exist *except* as parts of the one composite that is God.[35] In other words, he calls into question the presupposition that simplicity is ontologically superior to compositeness, which is the suppressed major premise of the argument. The real argument is that God, being first, which is to say ontologically superior, cannot have parts. With the removal of the suppressed major premise God could have parts and still be first if those parts were dependent on God and not God on the parts, or in other words, could not exist except as parts of God. The point is not that Hughes's proposal should be accepted as a viable alternative to the simplicity doctrine. Rather, since in the absence of the philosophical presupposition of the ontological superiority of simplicity over compositeness his counter proposal appears to be as equally plausible as its opposite,

---

Simplicity, 104–14.

35. Hughes, *Complex Theory*, 35–36. He writes, "It is still up for grabs whether God is in some sense posterior to some of his constituents, since any constituent would not be an individual substance distinct from God, and hence would not be (in the strict sense) *entia* prior to God" (36).

the suspicion is raised that neither position can be established and perhaps even that both are pseudo-propositions.

In the second variation, it is argued that, if God were composite, then an efficient cause would be required for the different parts to coalesce into the whole that is God, in which case God would no longer be first of all things. A composite exists because its efficient agent *already* exists.[36] Although it is often expressed using Aristotelian terminology, this argument is not dependent on an Aristotelian ontology for its validity; rather it is based on the common-sense axiom that a physical composite cannot be its own cause: a pre-existing cause is required for physical parts to coalesce into a whole.[37] (On this issue Aristotelianism reflects a common-sense view of causation.) An extrapolation is then made from physical composites to God as a purely metaphysical composite.[38] Aquinas states, "Now every composite has being through the union of its component parts. Therefore every composite depends on a pre-existing agent: and consequently the first being which is God, from whom all things proceed, cannot be composite" (*De potent.* 7.1).[39] What Aquinas means is that a composite thing of any type necessarily requires an agent to cause the different parts of it to be brought together to become a whole. God as the "first being" (*primum ens*), however, cannot be composite since there could be no agent on which God the first cause could be dependent (*De potent.* 7.1). Not even being a composite consisting of essence and existence is possible for God. If God is not both his essence and existence then God can only exist as caused by something other than himself and therefore cannot be the first efficient cause (*ST* 1.3.4; *SCG* 1.22).[40] In addition, unless God's essence is his existence, God would

---

36. A modern variant of this is to assert that God's unity results from God's freedom (Kaufman, *Systematic Theology. A Historicist Perspective*, 149–51).

37. See also *De ent. et ess.* 5.

38. Similarly, John Duns Scotus asserts that God as the first can have no efficient cause, for otherwise God would not be the first efficient cause (*primum efficiens*). Confusingly, however, he discusses only the possibility of God as a composite of matter and form, concluding that God cannot be a composite of matter and form because such a composite requires an efficient cause (*Ord.* 1.8.1.1, n. 7) (Cross, *Duns Scotus on God*, 99–114). It follows that if he exists, God cannot be a composite: "God is not composed of essential parts," but what Duns Scotus has in mind is the essential parts of matter and form (6). He also argues that God as immaterial can have no quantitative parts and that God cannot have spiritual accidents insofar as God's substance is his attributes.

39. See *SCG* 1.18.5.

40. The idea that God could cause his own existence is dismissed by Aquinas as impossible "by the constituent principles of that essence." He writes, "Now it is impossible

have potentiality, which would be impossible since potentiality can only be actualized through an efficient cause but God is the first efficient cause. Aquinas explains that essence relates to existence as potentiality relates to actuality: "Therefore existence must be compared to essence, if the latter is a distinct reality, as actuality to potentiality. Therefore, since in God there is no potentiality . . . it follows that in him essence does not differ from existence" (*ST* 1.3.4). Unless God's essence was his existence then God's essence would only be potentially existent and would therefore require an efficient cause to become actually existent. Finally, if he had existence by participation rather than essentially, God would no longer be the "first being" (*primum ens*), but a being that participates in the being of an ontologically prior entity. He writes, "If, therefore, he is not his own existence he will be not essential, but participated being. He will not therefore be the first being" (*ST* 1.3.4).[41] A similar argument is made from what is called God's independence (*independentia*). God could not be composite and be independent because as composite God would depend on an agent for his composition. It follows that if he exists at all, God can only be simple.[42]

The second variation of the argument for divine simplicity from God as first rests on the two questionable presuppositions that the concept of a metaphysical part is unitive and that extrapolation is possible from the

---

for a thing's existence to be caused by its essential constituent principles, for nothing can be the sufficient cause of its own existence, if its existence is caused." (*ST* 1.3.4). A thing cannot be its own efficient cause.

41. Paul Tillich agrees that God is being-itself, but gives this assertion an existentialist interpretation (*ST* I, part II, IIb, 3 235–41). As being-itself, God is not *a* being but the ground of being for beings, which is also expressed as "the power inherent in everything, the power of resisting nonbeing" (236). He modernizes the traditional view that God's essence is his existence, or that God is subsistent existence itself: "As being-itself God is beyond the contrast of essential and existential being. We have spoken of the transition of being into existence, which involves the possibility that being will contradict and lose itself. This transition is excluded from being-itself . . . for being-itself does not participate in nonbeing. In this it stands in contrast to every being. As classical theology has emphasized, God is beyond essence and existence" (236). This is the sole non-symbolic statement about God.

42. Quenstedt, *Theologia didactico-polemica sive systema theologicum*, cap. VIII; sect. II, quaest. V; Turretin, *Institutio Theologiae Elencticae*, locus tertius, quaest. VII.IV. Similarly, Turretin argues that what is composite is less perfect than what is not because the former presupposes "passive power, dependency and mutability" (potentiam passivam, dependentiam et mutabilitatem). What he seems to mean is that what is composite as a whole can still be acted upon by an agent or some of its parts may be liable to be acted upon by other parts. This means that the composite is dependent on what has brought its parts together or some of its parts are dependent upon other parts.

nature of a physical composite to that of a metaphysical composite. Even on the assumption of the validity of these two presuppositions, however, it can be argued that God could be composite without requiring an efficient cause. This second variation of the argument has for its major premise: Whatever does not require an efficient cause in order to exist is incomposite.[43] This premise is questionable because it is not obvious that being incomposite is a necessary correlate of not being caused by an efficient cause. Against the traditional position, Hughes argues plausibly that "a prior causal agent" may not be required for the existence of a composite having only metaphysical parts like God. He proposes that there may be two types of composites: contingently bound that need an efficient cause and necessarily bound that do not need an efficient cause.[44] Thus, it would seem that what is really decisive in the argument is the unstated presupposition that simplicity is ontologically superior to compositeness, with the result that it is impossible for what is first to be composite. This is not to say that Hughes counter proposal is convincing, but just that it is not unconvincing. The same objection applies to the argument for God's simplicity from his independence: it may be possible to be composite and still be independent. Given that the thesis and antithesis seem equally convincing, one suspects that on this issue one may have entered into a realm about which human beings know nothing.

In a third variation of the argument for divine simplicity from God as first, Bonaventure argues that, since God is "first in the genus of being" (*primum in genere entium*) and every first is the most simple, then God is the most simple of all beings (*Comm. sent.* I.8.2.1). This argument relies on the Aristotelean major premise that "by as much as something is first by so much is it more simple" (Aristotle, *Metaph.* 11.1). By first is meant ontologically first. To be first in the genus of being probably means that God is the first efficient cause by which all other things have their being, or is the source of the being of all other beings. It follows that God is most simple in the sense of being wholly simple. Bonaventure's argument from God as first admittedly depends upon the Aristotelian major premise that "by as much as something is first by so much is it more simple," which assumes both that there are degrees of being and that there is a necessary positive correlation between ontological priority and simplicity. To a non-Aristotelian,

---

43. Whatever does not require an efficient cause in order to exist is incomposite (ba); God (as the first) does not require an efficient cause in order to exist (cb); God is incomposite (ca).

44. Hughes, *Complex Theory*, 38–41.

the truth of such a premise is not obvious, and the proposition may even be dismissed as meaningless. Besides, the argument assumes that being can be considered a genus, which some Aristotelians, including Aquinas, reject.

From God as *Actus Purus*

As a corollary of being *actus purus*, which follows from being the first cause, Aquinas offers the thoroughly Aristotelian argument that God cannot be otherwise than simple. From the conclusion that God is the first mover, Aquinas infers that God is unmoving and unmovable, for otherwise God's motion would require an efficient cause and for that reason God would no longer be *first* mover.[45] Being unmovable means that God can have no potentiality, but is *actus purus*. In other words, in God as the first mover there can be no reduction of potentiality to act. Having no potentiality means that the first mover cannot be composite (*compositum*), by which is meant not merely having no compositeness of potentiality and actuality, but no compositeness of any type. What is being assumed is that to be composite is *necessarily* to have potentiality: compositeness and potentiality are correlates, being convertible. He writes, "For any composite being must contain two things that are related to each other as potentiality to act" (*Compend.* 1.9).[46] In his earlier *Quaestiones disputatae de potentia*, Aquinas puts forward three supports for the position that God is simple (7.1), the first of which explains more completely why being composite is necessarily to have potentiality. In a two-step process, he argues from God as pure act to the conclusion that God is necessarily simple. In step one, he sets forth the previously-proven assertion that, since act precedes potentiality in nature and in time, the first act (*actus primus*) must be pure act (*actus purus*), having no potentiality (1.1).[47] In the second step, he moves from God as pure act to God as necessarily simple. He states that the parts of any composite have potentiality in relation to one another. Matter is potential in relation to form, subject to its accidents, and genus to its specific differ-

---

45. Weigel, *Aquinas on Simplicity*, 103–35.

46. Nam in omni compositione oportet esse duo, quae ad invicem se habeant sicut potentia ad actum.

47. Aquinas writes, "Accordingly the being that made all things actual, and itself proceeds from no other being, must be the first actual being without any admixture of potentiality. For were it in any way in potentiality, there would be need of another previous being to make it actual."

ence. In addition, all the parts considered together are potential in relation to the whole, being matter to form.[48] By this he means that each of the parts is potentially part of a formally-identifiable whole before it actually becomes part of it.[49] Moreover, these parts even when belonging to a whole have potentiality to be separate or to be parts of other wholes. God, however, has no potentiality, from which it follows that God cannot have parts but can only be completely simple (*omnino simplex*).[50] His reasoning is that whatever is pure act has no potentiality and what has no potentiality has no compositeness because potentiality without parts is impossible insofar as it is a function of having parts. Aquinas concludes, "No composite is first act."[51] Similarly, Turretin states that God as *actus purissimus* is incomposite, with no admixture of potentiality. He writes, "From actuality, because God is most pure act, who has no admixture of potentiality."[52] He does not, however, provide the required Aristotelian argumentation for his conclusion, but merely assumes its validity.

The argument for God's simplicity from God as *actus purus* is clearly circular, being inextricably integrated within an Aristotelian cosmology. To a theologian who for whatever reason rejects the view that potentiality is part-like and so can be thought of as inhering in a substratum thereby making it composite, this argument is unpersuasive and even meaningless. Even on the assumption that the concepts of potentiality and actuality have real referents, as opposed to being merely pragmatically useful, however, it can legitimately be asked whether a concept such as God as *actus purus* is compatible with a Christian understanding of God, as Christian-Aristotelian theologians assume. That it is compatible is in fact counter-indicated by the absurd result that God as *actus purus*, which is supposed to follow

---

48. The same argument is stated more briefly in *Summa Theologiae*: "Because in every composite there must be potentiality and actuality; but this does not apply to God; for either one of the parts actuates another, or at least all the parts are potential to the whole" (1.3.7).

49. What is required is an efficient cause to bring the parts together into a composite, thereby actualizing their potentiality.

50. Augustine identifies the triune God as the simple, unchangeable Good by which all composite, changeable goods have been created (*Civ. Dei* XI.10). He writes, "There is, accordingly, a Good which is alone simple (*bonum solum simplex*), and therefore alone unchangeable, and this is God. By this Good have all others been created, but not simple, and therefore not unchangeable."

51. Nullum compositum potest esse actus primus.

52. Turretin, *Institutio Theologiae Elencticae*, locus tertius, quaest. VII.IV. He writes, "Ab actuositate, quia Deus est actus purissimus qui nullam habet potentiam admixtam."

necessarily from God as first cause, would be incapable of entering into relations with his own creation. Of course, Aristotle has no problems with this conclusion, since his God is not a creator and is eternally isolated from all other things, only thinking about thinking (*Metaph.* 12.9; 1075 34). But a Christian theologian who is committed to the biblical portrayal of God as creator and interactive with his creation could not without detrimental qualification embrace Aristotle's insular concept of God. Moreover, that Hughes can argue for the opposite conclusion from the same Aristotelian premises further undermines the persuasiveness of the argument. He reasons that if potentiality is defined broadly enough God could be said to have potentiality.[53] If it is possible to distinguish a receiver from that which it receives in order for it to be "a certain kind of individual, or be a certain way, or be," then God can be said to be in potentiality to his essence. Hughes writes, "And a thing is in some way in potentiality if and only if it can be as it were 'factored' into a receiving element and a (distinct) received element."[54] If God can be said to be potential even in this minimalistic sense, then the argument to God as necessarily simple from God as *actus purus* is no longer viable.[55] The only reason that one may reject the conception of God

---

53. Hughes, *Complex Theory*, 41–50.

54. Ibid., 46.

55. Arguing for the opposite position, Mullins claims that simplicity is not metaphysically compossible with the nature of God because being simple necessitates that God be without freedom and to be without freedom is not to be God ("Simply Impossible: A Case against Divine Simplicity."). The reason for this is that, since being simple entails having no potentiality, being pure act, it follows that God could not have created otherwise than he did ("states of affairs" and "possible worlds"), insofar as God would have had no potentiality. Mullins writes, "The Triune God is perfectly free, and freedom, as I shall argue, is not compossible with pure act. One should recall that as pure act God has no unactualized potential. If God has any unactualized potential, He is not simple." He considers such a view to be unacceptable because "it denies of God his infinite creative freedom and sovereignty over creation" and because it denies God's aseity: "In order for God to be who He is—pure act—He necessarily must create this world. This makes God's essential nature dependent upon creation." He refers to God's lack of freedom in relation to this world and other possible worlds as "modal collapse." Mullins's argument, however, is only effective against those who are theologically audacious enough to espouse the view of God's absolute freedom; it is not effective against those who are willing to put some limitations on what God could or could not do based upon the divine nature, such as the impossibility of God's creating an evil universe, which Mullins himself accepts. The difference between Mullins and the advocates of the simplicity doctrine is only relative, the latter imposing an additional limitation upon God than the former. Advocates of the simplicity doctrine would accept the consequence that God creates with no unactualized potentiality, including the very act of creating, and so has no creative freedom. As such

The Oneness and Simplicity of God

as having a type of potentiality would be because one tacitly presupposes that simplicity is ontologically superior to compositeness.

From God as Most Noble

To be ranked as more noble than something else is to be recognized as ontologically superior, which presupposes that there are gradations of being. From the premise that God is most noble (*nobilissimus*), it is argued that God is most simple on the assumption of a correlation between simplicity and ontological superiority. Aquinas holds as axiomatic that the more simple something is the more noble it is, as, for example, in the genus of the hot, fire, with no mixture of cold, is the most noble of all hot things. With respect to God, the criterion of nobility is causative power: the more something is a cause, rather than an effect, the more noble it is. Thus God as *first* cause is nobler than all created things, which are effects of the first cause. From this the conclusion follows that God is simple since simplicity is a necessary correlate of nobility, being convertible with it. Aquinas writes, "That, therefore, which is at the peak of nobility (*in fine nobilitatis*) among all beings must be at the peak of simplicity (*in fine simplicitatis*). But the being that is at the peak of nobility among all beings we call God, since he is the first cause. For a cause is nobler than an effect. God can, therefore, have no composition" (*SCG* 1.18.6).[56] Similarly, in another work Aquinas argues that God as the first principle of being (*primum principium essendi*) possesses being in the noblest manner insofar as God is his own being (*Sent.* 8.4.1).[57] But this is not true of any composite, since a composite consists of parts that are not being-itself (*ipsum esse*). In this context not to be being-itself is the result of being a part: because it is a part, each part of a whole derives its being from the composite of which it is a part. God as his own being, insofar as he has no parts, is being-itself. Likewise, on the assumption that "simplicity is the condition of nobility," Bonaventure asserts that God is most simple because God is most noble (*Comm. sent.*

---

they would hold either that God created this world because it was the best possible world, the one most consistent with divine perfection, or that God created all possible worlds, a multiverse. Either option allows God to have no potentiality—to be pure act—and so be simple.

56. Aquinas explains that it is better that the divine goodness to be in one thing rather than many (*ST* 1.3.7).

57. Deus est suum esse.

I.8.2.1).[58] This assumes gradations of being of being with simplicity as the criterion.

Many modern philosophers would reject as meaningless the so-called axiom that the more simple something the more noble it is, since this requires that there be gradations of being. Rather, in a more philosophically egalitarian spirit, it is thought that something is or it is not and any ranking of beings is purely subjective. On the assumption that it is meaningful to distinguish more and less noble types of beings, however, to say that God cannot be otherwise than simple because God is most noble does not follow. This is because it is not obvious that simplicity and nobility are necessary correlates and convertible; rather such an assertion rests on the implicit presupposition that simplicity is ontologically superior to compositeness, which is not self-evident. In fact, if anything, one would expect that, based on analogy with human experience, complexity and nobility should be correlates. For example, the less complex an organism is the less advanced it is and therefore the less noble it is thought to be. Aquinas' own concept of the contraction of being would suggest this view since the less contracted a thing is the more complex and the closer to being itself it is (see *ST* 1.44.2).

From God as Infinite

It is argued that the fact that God is infinite in the sense of being without limits entails that God is simple; this argument is most closely associated with John Duns Scotus.[59] According to him, God is infinite, and every infinite being is incomposite, from which it follows that God is incomposite (*Ord.* 1.8.1, nn. 17, 19).[60] Proof for the major premise that every infinite being is incomposite follows from the absurdity of conceiving God, who is infinite, as composite. Duns Scotus reasons that, on the hypothesis that God is composite, God's parts would be either finite or infinite. If the former then God would be finite, not infinite, since the infinite exceeds the finite infinitely: no amount of finite parts could ever equal an infinite whole. If the latter, then a part would be equally as infinite as the whole and so could not be exceeded (*excedi*). The result would be that a part would not be less

---

58. Simplicitas est conditio nobilitatis.

59. Cross, *Duns Scotus on God*, 99–114.

60. In a prayer, John Duns Scotus addresses God as following: "You are the ultimate in simplicity, having no really distinct parts, or no realities in your essence which are not really the same" (*DPP* 4.84).

The Oneness and Simplicity of God

than the whole of which it is a part, but this is a contradiction given the nature of a part. Underlying this argument is Duns Scotus's view that, because it is less than the whole to which it belongs, a part must be finite and as such be capable of being exceeded. He explains, "Every component part can be part of some total composite which is from it and another component; every part can be exceeded (*excedi*)" (*Ord.* 1.8.1.1, n. 17).[61] Moreover, on the assumption that the infinite is the perfect, having perfect identity, the result of adding a part to the infinite would be that God becomes more perfect, which is impossible (*Ord.* 1.8.1.1, n. 18).[62] Along the same lines, in *De prima principia*, on the hypothesis that God is a composite, Duns Scotus sets forth a disjunction, both elements of which he rejects as untenable. He writes, "If the essence were composed its components would be in themselves either finite or infinite. In the first case, the composite would be finite, in the second a part would not be less than the whole" (*DPP* 4.76). Two possibilities exist for a composite. Either it is composed of finite parts in which case it would be a finite composite. Or it is composed of infinite parts, but this is absurd since an infinite part would not be less than the infinite whole, which is a contradiction, given the nature of a part. It follows that no composite can be infinite.[63]

61. Quod omne componibile potest esse pars alicuius totius compositi quod est ex ipso et alio componibili; omnis autem pars potest excedi.

62. Duns Scotus's auxiliary argument from God as infinite to God as incomposite relies upon the theological correlate of God's perfection. First, he argues that the infinite is perfect and as such has in itself perfect identity: it is what it is completely (*Ord.* 1.8.1.1, n. 18). He writes, "No infinite lacks that with which it can be in some way the same, indeed it has every such in itself according to perfect identity (Nullum infinitum caret eo cum quo potest esse aliquo modo idem, immo omne tale habet in se secundum perfectam identitatem)." He seems to be implying that a composite cannot have perfect identity because its parts are neither identical to the whole nor to one another; what cannot have perfect identity is not perfect, but God is perfect. Second, continuing his argument, Duns Scotus says that, if the infinite could be combined with a part, the result would be that the infinite with the addition of a part would be more perfect than the infinite alone. The idea of a more perfect infinite, however, is contradictory: "It is against the notion of the infinite that it can be understood to be more perfect or that there is something more perfect than it (Contra rationem autem infiniti simipliciter est quod ipsum posset intelligi perfectius vel aliquid perfectius eo)." The conclusion follows that because it is perfect the infinite cannot be a composite.

63. Duns Scotus presents another argument in favor of God's simplicity: based on the assumptions that what understands cannot be extended and that what is unextended is simple, he argues that God is simple because God understands (*DPP* 4.79). This argument, however, does not prove that God is uniquely simple. Bonaventure offers another version of the argument for God's simplicity from God's infinity. Beginning from the assumptions

Samuel Clarke likewise holds that God's simplicity follows from God's infinity: to be infinite entails having no parts.[64] He begins his argument from the premise of God as self-existent, which he assumes requires no proof. To be self-existent is to exist by an absolute necessity in the nature of the thing itself. For this to be true, however, a being must be infinite, insofar as only the infinite exists independently and of itself. The reason for this is that if a being were an effect of something it would be limited by it; as a result it would be finite, not infinite. (He adds that whatever is self-existent must also be eternal.) Clarke then proceeds from God's infinity to God's simplicity by arguing that the infinity of the self-existent must be one of "fullness and immensity," by which is meant, not only being without limits, but also without "diversity, defect or interruption." In addition, the self-existent must be "most simple, unchangeable and incorruptible, without parts, figure, motion, divisibility or any other such properties as we find in matter."[65] Although he does not clearly explain why there is this necessary connection between infinity and simplicity, it seems that for Clarke not to have any of the properties enumerated is to have limitations, or what he calls "bounds," which are incompatible with the boundless infinite. He seems to assume that God must be the opposite of what material things are, so that if the latter are composite then the former is simple.

Duns Scotus's argument from God's infinity to God's simplicity assumes that a metaphysical part is generically identical to a physical part, so that what is true of the latter is true of the former. A physical composite, or a magnitude (*magnitudo*), is the sum of its physical parts, which by definition are finite and therefore can "be exceeded" (*excedi*). For this reason they are less than the whole to which they belong; by "less" in this case he means both quantitatively and formally less. Duns Scotus holds that there cannot be a quantitative infinite, so that any infinite thing would have to be incorporeal, or a spirit, and its parts therefore could only be

---

that a correlation exists between degrees of simplicity and degrees of being powerful in virtue (*virtus*), by which seems to be meant God's greatness, and that the greater the virtue of something the simpler it is, Bonaventure argues that, because God is infinite in virtue, God is therefore most simple (*Comm. sent.* I.8.2.1). In the Scholium that follows, Bonaventure includes actuality as a correlative of God's simplicity, in order to distinguish God, who is *summe simplex* (most highly simple), from other lesser types of simplicity, namely that of prime matter, which is complete potentiality and said to be *simpliciter simplex* (simply simple), being only the privation of composition. Bonaventure does not provide proof, however, that virtue (*virtus*) and simplicity are necessary correlates.

64. Clarke, *Discourse concerning the Being and Attributes of God*, 44–47.
65. Ibid., 45.

metaphysical parts (*Ord.* 1.8.1.1, nn. 10–13). Nevertheless, what is true of a physical composite is true of a metaphysical one: it must always be finite. The question that needs to be raised is whether physical and metaphysical parts can be understood as generically identical. As already indicated, it seems naïve to assume that a metaphysical part is a part at all, except in a borrowed and metaphorical sense, and even that it is a unitive concept, except superficially.

Even on the assumption of the validity of the concept of a metaphysical part, it is possible that the axiom that every part can be exceeded need not apply to an infinite being. Perhaps one could argue that God's metaphysical parts are such that they alone cannot be exceeded. If so, then God is an infinite whole with infinite parts. There are no doubt many differences between a finite and an infinite being, and this may be one of them. This is not to say that God is an infinite whole with infinite parts, but only to set up an equally plausible antithesis to the thesis that an infinite being cannot have parts. The purpose of this thought experiment is to demonstrate that such questions may transcend the scope of legitimate theologizing. In fact, it would seem that the presupposition that simplicity is ontologically superior to compositeness is the real, but undisclosed basis of Duns Scotus's argument from God as infinite to God as incomposite.

Rather than equating it with infinity and by extension simplicity, as Duns Scotus does, perfection could be defined in such a way that allows for compositeness. It is equally possible to hold the position that God's perfection results from being a fully-actualized composite consisting of a limited number of infinite attributes.[66] God is not perfect because he is infinite and simple, but because he lacks no essential attribute. Such a definition is at least more consistent with a common sense understanding of perfection: based on analogy with human experience, being perfect with perfect identity results from the perfect integration of parts. Those who adopt such a position would agree with Duns Scotus that the addition of a part to God would result contradictorily in God's being more perfect than God, but for

---

66. A possible objection to God as infinite having a finite number of attributes is that being infinite may imply having an infinitive number of attributes, as Spinoza asserts. In his *Ethics*, he writes, "The more reality or being a thing has the greater the number of its attributes" (I Prop ix). He concludes that an infinite substance must have infinite attributes, presumably because not to do so would a contradiction, for it would mean that the infinite is limited, which is to say, finite. This follows from the unstated premise that attributes exist in proportion to degree of reality; infinite reality therefore entails infinite attributes. If God has infinite attributes then God is unknowable since to know a finite number is still not to know an infinite number of attributes.

Traditional Argumentation for the Simplicity Doctrine

a different reason. It is not that God could have no part at all because God is perfect with perfect identity, but that no part could be added to a fully-actualized, or perfect, composite. One could even argue that what Duns Scotus describes as perfect is so homogenous, insofar as it is simple, that it transcends the category of perfection altogether, so that to call God perfect is equivocation.

Samuel Clark's assumption that what is infinite is simple because attributes or properties would function as bounds is not at all self-evident. It seems equally as plausible to argue that to be without limits is actually to be inclusive of all limits and so be the most composite of all beings: infinite means unlimited, all-inclusive diversity. Therefore, since both positions can be defended, it seems that the question of whether God is simple because God is infinite may be a pseudo-question, the type that a theologian should eschew.

Finally, it should be noted that in Scripture God is never explicitly said to be infinite; rather infinity is an implied attribute of God or a mode of each of the attributes of God (infinitely wise or powerful, etc.). Even if it is theologically advisable to describe God as infinite, it might be better to take this in an apophatic sense of being other than all things, which, as particular things, are by definition finite. In other words, God as infinite is not to be conceived as a being at all, not even an unlimited being.[67] On such an understanding of infinity the inference of divine simplicity is not possible.

From God as Perfect

God's simplicity is said to follow from God's perfection. Although it depends in part on the philosophical presuppositions of the theologian using the concept, perfection means generally the state of being the best possible. In Aristotelian philosophy perfection more precisely is said to be act proper to subject, which is to say, a subject that is fully what it is essentially.[68] In the case of God, there are no limits on perfection. There are three versions of the argument for God's simplicity from God's perfection.

First, on the assumption that God is whatever it is better to be than not to be, it is argued without recourse to Aristotelian philosophical categories

---

67. Smith, *The Indescribable God*, 121–40.

68. God's perfection is affirmed in Scripture (see Job 37:16; Matt 5:48; Pss 90; 102; 1 Sam 15:29; Rom 1:23) See Heidegger, *Corpus theologiae christianae*, locus tertius, xxxii). Its meaning in Scripture, however, is moral perfection, not metaphysical.

The Oneness and Simplicity of God

that, since to be incomposite is better than being composite, God is incomposite. The reason that it is better to be incomposite than composite is that to be the latter is to be liable to being destroyed through decomposition. Anselm writes, "But to be many and not one, or to be capable of dissolution even in thought is far from your nature, since you are that than which no better can be conceived" (*Prosl.* 18). Based on Anselm's description of God as "that than which nothing greater can be conceived," the notion of a composite God is a contradiction.[69] Likewise, Lutheran scholastic theologian Amandus Polanus argues that for God to be perfect is inconsistent with being liable to non-being, or destruction. Since the more composite something is the more liable it is to non-being, it follows that God as perfect cannot be composite at all. He puts forth as self-evident the principle that the more perfect a thing is, the more simple it is.[70]

The argument that, because he is perfect, it is better for God to be simple than composite assumes that a metaphysical part is a unitive concept and that, because it is generically identical to a physical part, what is true of the latter is true of the former. A physical composite is liable to decomposition and the more parts a composite has the more liable it is to it. By extension, the same is said to be true of a non-physical composite consisting of metaphysical parts. However, even on the assumption that a metaphysical part is a valid concept, there is no reason to think that a non-physical composite necessarily is liable to non-physical decomposition; a physical and metaphysical part could differ in this respect. It is not contradictory to think of a non-physical composite as invulnerable to decomposition and so as eternal and necessary. Moreover, based on analogy with human experience, of the two concepts of God, it could be argued that it is better for God to be composite than simple. A human being, for example, is better than a single-celled organism, so by extension God as perfect must be maximally complex. Another criticism of the argument is that it assumes the validity of what is known as "perfect being theology," according to which, even though he is maximally great, God differs from created things only in degree, not absolutely. This oddly would apply even to God's simplicity: God is only more simple than other less simple, created things, rather than being absolutely different from them insofar as

---

69. Feinberg, *No One Like Him*, 327.

70. Polanus, *Syntagma theologiae christianae*, lib. 2, caput IIX. He writes, "Quo perfectius esse aliquid habet, eo logius abest a non esse, et proinde a divisione, quae east via ad non esse. In quo libet rerum genere tanto aliquid est perfectius, quanto etiam simplicius."

Traditional Argumentation for the Simplicity Doctrine

he is simple. In other words, simplicity is no longer a divine distinctive.[71] Perfect being theology, however, even though it attributes maximally great-making properties to him, severely and detrimentally anthropomorphizes God, and for that reason should be rejected as a theological option.

Second, it is argued that something cannot be most perfect if it is composed of parts since the parts necessarily are less perfect than the whole by virtue of being parts. So if God is most perfect then God must be simple.[72] Aquinas explains, "For parts are imperfect in comparison with the whole. . . . If, then, God is composite, his proper perfection and goodness is found in the whole, not in any part of the whole. Thus, there will not be in God purely that good which is proper to him. God, then, is not the first and highest good" (*SCG* 1.18.7). The argument is that God cannot be supremely good and composite at the same time. The reason for this is that the parts of a composite thing are never as perfect as the whole of which they are parts; if they were, then they would not be parts of something greater and more perfect than themselves.[73] In other words, to have parts is to have some degree of imperfection corresponding to the amount of composition. If he were composite, God could not be said to be supremely perfect by being the highest good. In another expression of the argument, Aquinas argues that God as the first being must be a most perfect being (*esse perfectissimum*) and for that reason supremely good (*optimum*). If supremely good, God cannot be lacking in any goodness. From this it follows that God cannot be dependent upon parts that separately are not supremely good, which would be the case if God were composite; the parts, by virtue of being parts and not the whole, would be less good than the whole. He writes, "But this is impossible in any composite thing because the good that results from the composition of its parts, and whereby the whole is good, is not in any single part" (*De poten.* 7).[74] It follows that only the supremely simple can be supremely good: the latter cannot be composed of parts that in themselves are not supremely good.

The argument of the incompatibility of God's having parts with God's supreme perfection and goodness relies on the Aristotelian concept that a part is ontologically less perfect than the whole of which it is a part.

71. Miller, *A Most Unlikely God*, 1–4.

72. Weigel, *Aquinas on Simplicity*, 169–71.

73. Hughes, *Complex Theory*, 3–59.

74. Hoc autem in nullo composito est possibile. Nam bonum quod resultat ex compositione partium, per quod totum est bonum, non inest alicui partium.

The Oneness and Simplicity of God

However, for the one who is not an Aristotelian, to consider something as more or less perfect may be meaningless. A part is not less perfect by virtue of being a part, but simply is what it is, a part of a whole. What really informs argument seems to be the tacit presupposition that simplicity is ontologically superior to compositeness. In addition, the argument is one of extrapolation based on analogy with created things, either physical or non-physical. It is assumed that the fewer parts a thing has the more perfection it has insofar as it is more uniformly itself and less dependent on what it is not. As applied to God there is a qualitative leap made from fewest parts to no parts.[75] It is questionable, however, whether in this context a being with no parts is even conceivable. God as simple is actually something of the limit-case of the relation of parts to the whole: a being that has no parts but is only a whole. In other words, God does not belong to the series of things that have variously more or fewer parts. For this reason, it is doubtful that supreme perfection and goodness can be attributed without equivocation to something that is different in kind from things that have more or less degrees of perfection and goodness depending on the number of their parts. It could in fact be argued that a thing is its parts when those parts are essential to it, so that to conceive of a being that is more perfect by virtue of not depending on parts at all makes no sense. If God as simple is an exception to the analytical truth that a thing is its essential parts, then no argument from analogy can be used to prove that, since the fewer parts something has the more perfect it is, God as that which has no parts must be supremely perfect. Having no parts, God becomes other than all composite things. Finally, if anything, as already indicated, it would seem that perfection would be expressed more in complexity than in simplicity, on the assumption that the more composite a thing is the more inclusive of all being it is, or to use Aquinas's terminology the less contracted its being is.

Third it is argued that God cannot be the most perfect being unless God is simple since to be simple is intrinsically better than being composite. Charnock considers it to be axiomatic that "the more perfect anything is in the rank of creatures, the more spiritual and simple it is."[76] As a rule the more perfect a created being is the more simple it is.[77] For example,

---

75. Hughes, *Complex Theory*, 41.

76. Charnock, *The Complete Works of Stephen Charnock*, vol. 1, *Discourses on Divine Providence and The Existence and Attributes of God*, 268.

77. Zanchi writes, "In quolibetrerum genere, tanto aliquid est perfectius et noblius, quanto etiam est simplicius et purius" (*De Natura Dei, De Attributis*, lib. 2, cap. 2).

the fewer impurities a piece of gold has the more perfect it is.[78] So by extrapolation God as most perfect must be most simple, which is to say, wholly simple. Zanchi explains that God is the most perfect of all beings because God is the being of being and cause of causes (*ens entium, et causa causarum*), which apparently means that God is simple.[79] (For this reason God can only be spiritual since all bodies are composite.) This argument presupposes the supposed necessary truth that simplicity is ontologically superior to compositeness and so is intrinsically better. Again, however, if anything, it would seem that complexity in unity is intrinsically better than the bare unity of simplicity (a Hegelian insight)—certainly it is more valued by human beings.

From God as Necessary

The simplicity of God is said to be inferable from the necessity of God, insofar as what is composite can never be necessary. As Aquinas explains, since God is a necessary being (*per se necesse-esse*) God cannot be composite since no composite is necessary inasmuch as every composite is potentially dissoluble (*dissolubile*) and therefore can not-be (*in potentia ad non esse*) (SCG 1.18).[80] Likewise, John Duns Scotus argues that God is a necessary being and every necessary being is simple (*Ord.* 1.8.1.1). According to him, to be necessary is to be *ex se*, independent of all things for existence. Proof that whatever is necessary is simple is as follows. On the one hand, a necessary being cannot be composite because if part A is possible (*possibile-esse*) and part B necessary (*necesse-esse*), then the composite will not be necessary because necessary existence will be composed of possible existence, which is a contradiction. In particular, the relation between part A and part B will not be necessary if part A is possible. On the other hand, if part A is necessary, it will be from itself the highest degree of actuality (*ultima actualitate*) insofar as it is necessary. It follows that part A as the highest degree of actuality cannot become more than it already is by virtue of being a part of a whole. He writes, "If A is of itself necessary existence, then it is of

---

78. Charnock, *The Complete Works of Stephen Charnock*, vol. 1, *Discourses on Divine Providence and The Existence and Attributes of God*, 268; Zanchi, *De Natura Dei, De Attributis*, lib. 2, cap. 2.

79. Zanchi, *De Natura Dei, De Attributis*, lib. 2, cap. 2.

80. Hughes questions the validity of Aquinas's arguments that God must lack potentiality (*Complex Theory*, 6–50).

itself in ultimate actuality, and so with nothing can it make itself to be *per se* one thing."[81] Moreover, Duns Scotus explains that if both part A and part B are necessary, then the composite will be doubly necessary. In other words, if A as necessary and B as necessary are a composite and B is removed from A, A will still be necessary. This he finds to be impossible, although he does not explain why, except perhaps because he holds that it is redundant and over-explained.[82]

Aquinas's view that every composite is dissoluble is an extrapolation from the nature of physical composites. Ordinary experience indicates that composites consisting of physical parts are dissoluble since the parts can be separated from one another. This conclusion is extended to all types of composites. The weakness of the argument is its assumption that a metaphysical part is a unitive concept and that it is analogous to a physical part insofar as it is generically identical. Even if there is such a thing as a composite consisting of metaphysical parts, however, there is still no reason to think that those metaphysical parts are dissoluble like physical parts would be. Rather it is just as possible to conceive of God as a necessary composite consisting of metaphysical parts. Again it would seem that what is being tacitly presupposed is that simplicity is ontologically superior to compositeness; the real argument seems to be that it is unworthy of God to be composed of parts, even metaphysical parts. Duns Scotus's argument is equally unpersuasive since he assumes that necessary parts cannot co-exist in a composite, but there seems to be nothing contradictory about a composite consisting of necessary parts. This is not to say that God is such a composite but only that the opposite hypothesis can be entertained without absurdity. In view of this, it may be better not even to consider the question of whether God as necessary is simple, since it seems to be theologically out of bounds.

From God as Immortal or Incorruptible

Closely related to the argument from necessity is the argument for divine simplicity from God's immorality or incorruptibility. Since a condition of mortality or corruptibility is being dissoluble into component parts, it follows that whatever is immortal or incorruptible must be incomposite.

81. Si a est ex se necesse esse, ergo est ex se ultima actualitate, et ita cum nullo facit per se unum.

82. Perhaps he is influenced by his view that there cannot be two infinite beings, as argued in *DPP* 3.23–24.

Novatian writes, "And what is immortal, whatever it is, that very thing is one and simple, and forever. And thus because it is one it cannot be dissolved; since whatever is that very thing which is placed beyond the claim of dissolution, it is freed from the laws of death"[83] (*De Trin.* 6). According to him, whatever is composite is decomposable into its parts and thereby destroyed. Since he is immortal, God cannot be destroyed, so, whatever else remains unknown about him, at least this much is known about God: that he is simple. Likewise, Athananius connects being incomposite with possessing existence, presumably because what is incomposite is indestructible. He writes, "But God possesses existence and is not composite" (*Adv. gent.* 3.41).[84] According to Anselm, by definition God cannot be composite since to be incomposite is better than being composite insofar as to be the latter is to be liable to being destroyed through decomposition, either actually or in thought. He writes, "For whatsoever is composed of parts is not in all respects one, but in a certain respect many and diverse from itself; and either actually or in thought can be dissolved (et vel actu vel intellectu dissolvi potest): but to be many and not one, or to be capable of dissolution even in thought is far from your nature, since you are that than which no better can be conceived" (*Prosl.* 18).[85]

To be dissoluble in thought is not an ontological defect, unless one presupposes, as Anselm does, that multiplicity in itself is ontologically inferior to simplicity. The view that it is may be called into question as a self-evident and indubitable truth. To be dissoluble in actuality, however, could more believably be viewed as an indicator of ontological inferiority. What is not taken into consideration, however, is the possibility that a composite being could also be immortal or incorruptible.[86] If so, then God could be composite and still be God. This is not to say that God is composite rather than simple, but only that it would not be contrary to the nature of God as immortal or incorruptible to be composite. One should perhaps suspect that neither has any applicability to God.

---

83. Quod enim immortale est, quicquid est, illud ipsum unum et simplex et semper est. Et ideo quia unum est, dissolui non potest, quoniam quicquid est illud ipsum extra ius dissolutionis positum, legibus est mortis solutum.

84. ὁ δὲ θεὸς ὤν ἐστι, καὶ οὐ σύνθετος.

85. Visser and Williams, *Anselm*, part II.

86. Hughes, *Complex Theory*, 36–38.

4

Recent Defense of the Simplicity Doctrine

EVEN THOUGH ENSHRINED IN historical Articles of Faith, the simplicity doctrine in the modern period has faded from the prominence that it formerly enjoyed, sometimes being judged to be a piece of scholastic arcanity. In some cases it was quietly dropped from theological treatises on the divine attributes. In other cases, the doctrine is explicitly rejected or reinterpreted. Since they are not derived from the feeling of absolute dependence, Schleiermacher, for example, methodologically rejects the doctrines of God's unity, infinity, and simplicity as meaningless.[1] Likewise, neo-orthodox theologian Emil Brunner dismisses the traditional doctrine of divine simplicity and immutability found in medieval and Protestant scholastic theology as contrary to the depiction of God in the Bible.[2] The Lutheran theologian Isaak Dorner gives the simplicity doctrine a Hegelian reinterpretation along the lines of the concept of the true infinite.[3]

---

1. Schleiermacher, *The Christian Faith*, § 56.

2. Brunner, *The Christian Doctrine of* God, 293-94. He dismisses the traditional doctrine of divine simplicity found in the so-called "older theologies."

3. "Durch Vermittlung der Vielheit der Eigenschaften die Einfachheit über eine bloß negative Bedeutung hinausgehoben werden kann. Das wird dann der Fall sein, wenn sich ergibt: Daß die göttliche Einfachheit nicht als abstracte leere Identität mit sich, nicht als das leere, reine Sein, das vom Nichts kaum zu unterscheiden wäre, gedacht warden darf. Sie wird vielmehr mit der Fülle der göttlichen Bestimmtheiten vereinbar sein müssen. Umgekehrt, diese Vielheit wird so zu denken sein, daß die Unterschiede, die in dem Begriff des einen absoluten Wesens sich uns zeigen werden, der gediegenen, absoluten Einheit Gottes nicht widersprechen, sondern sie bestätigen, indem sie von ihm ewig zur inneren Harmonie mit sich selbst zurückgeführt sind" (Dorner, *System der Christlichen Glaubenslehre*, vol. 1, *Grundlegung oder Apologetik*, 223).

Plantinga's Repudiation of the Simplicity Doctrine

A relatively recent assault on the simplicity doctrine has come from Alvin Plantinga, a Christian theologian trained in analytic philosophy.[4] Taking Aquinas's version of the doctrine as representative, he argues that the assertion that God is simple comes into conflict with other central Christian distinctives, in particular the tenets that God is a creator and a person.[5] According to him, it was meant to protect against two equally undesirable theological extremes: that God has no nature, a form of agnosticism, and that God is not sovereign or *a se*, self-existent. While he agrees with what he calls the sovereignty-aseity intuition behind it, Plantinga nevertheless rejects the simplicity doctrine as incoherent. First, the property-deity identification of the simplicity doctrine is incoherent. According to him, it is impossible to hold that God is identical to his properties (collectively, his nature), including existence, since this would mean that God is a property and not a person. He writes,

> If God is identical with each of his properties, then, since each of his properties is a property, he is a property—a self-exemplifying property. Accordingly, God has just one property: himself. This view is subject to a difficulty both obvious and overwhelming. No property could have created the world; no property could be omniscient, or, indeed, know anything at all. If God is a property, then he isn't a person but a mere abstract object; he has no knowledge, awareness, power, love, or life. So taken, the simplicity doctrine seems an utter mistake.[6]

If God is a person, a type of concrete object, God cannot at the same time be a property, an abstract object.[7] (By "person" Plantinga seems to

---

4. Plantinga, *Does God Have a Nature?* For criticism of the simplicity doctrine not long before Plantinga's work, see Bennett, "The Divine Simplicity"; LaCroix, "Augustine on the Simplicity of God"; Martin, "God, the Null Set and Divine Simplicity"; Morreall, "Divine Simplicity and Divine Properties"; Wainwright, "Augustine on God's Simplicity: A Reply." It should not be thought that philosophers and theologians were unaware of the problems with the simplicity doctrine before the rise of analytical philosophy.

5. See Gale, *On the Nature and Existence of God*, 23–29; Sadler, *Simply Divine: Simplicity as Fundamental to the Nature of God*, 128–30.

6. Plantinga, *Does God Have a Nature?*, 47.

7. Mann explains Plantinga's view: "Recall that chief among Plantinga's criticisms is the claim that the property view transforms God into a property, a bloodless abstract object that could not have created the world, care for us, and so forth ("Simplicity and Properties: A Reply to Morris," 352).

The Oneness and Simplicity of God

mean a consciousness, or mind, with thoughts, beliefs, and intentions.) Plantinga assumes that what exists is either abstract objects, which is to say, properties, or concrete objects that exemplify properties, which is to say, individuals. It is clear that his view assumes the property account of predication: if x is F then x's F-ness is a property. It follows that, if God exists, then God must be a concrete object and so to identify God with his properties or even one property, as the simplicity doctrine does, is nonsensical.[8] God cannot be a property because properties are exemplifiable by concrete objects; to identify God as a person (i.e., subject) with a property (i.e., predicate) is a category mistake: confusing an exemplifiable thing (abstract object) with a non-exemplifiable thing (concrete object).[9] Second, the property-property identity of the simplicity doctrine is also incoherent. According to Plantinga, the identification of each divine property with every other divine property is counterintuitive.[10] He writes,

> If God is identical with each of his properties, then each of his properties is identical with each of his properties, so that God has but one property. This seems flatly incompatible with the obvious fact that God has several properties; he has power and mercifulness, say, neither of which is identical with the other.[11]

In support of Plantinga's critique, it is further noted that, on the assumption that increasing degrees of a property become more distinctive, one would expect the differences between God's properties to be even more pronounced since they are of an unlimited degree.[12] If so, then the property-property identity becomes even less plausible.

According to Plantinga, the problems with the simplicity doctrine cannot be resolved by saying that God is identical not to his properties but to his *having* properties, in which case God would be identical to the state of affairs of his having properties.[13] The reason that shifting properties to

---

8. Holding such a position implicitly commits him to some version of substance theology: God is a substance, entity or being.

9. Hughes, *Complex Theory*, 62–63. He writes, "But the idea of a property that is its own and only its own property certainly looks incoherent" (63).

10. See Morreall, "Divine Simplicity and Divine Properties." He writes, "What Aquinas would have to provide to save his argument here is some explanation of how, in fact, all the property words we predicate of God have the same meaning. I do not see how this can be done without telling us what that meaning is" (69).

11. Plantinga, *Does God Have a Nature?*, 47.

12. Gale, *On the Nature and Existence of God*, 24.

13. Plantinga, *Does God Have a Nature?*, 48–53.

states of affairs is ineffective is because, first, the properties belonging to God's states of affairs would still be independent of God and, second, God would still be an abstract object and not a person.[14] Plantinga is likewise not open to the possibility that, because knowledge of God is only analogical and therefore partly discontinuous with knowledge of created things, it may be possible to hold that God is both a property and a person in some incomprehensible way.[15] In other words, he is unsympathetic to apophatic theology, viewing it as a type of agnosticism.

Plantinga's analytical philosophical work has generated many responses from those who seek to uphold some version of the simplicity doctrine. The effect of his work has been to initiate new discussion and prompt new defenses of it. One could say that the simplicity doctrine has thereby had somewhat of a resurgence of support. Modern Thomistic theologians in particular have a lot at stake in defending it because of the prominence that divine simplicity has in Aquinas's deduction of the attributes of God from God as first cause in his *Summa Theologiae*.[16] There are four different approaches adopted by those have undertaken to defend the simplicity doctrine against Plantinga's refutation of it.

Four Approaches to the Defense of the Simplicity Doctrine

Approach One: God as Valid Exception

Several philosophers and theologians defend the simplicity doctrine against Plantinga's attack of it by making God a valid exception to the rule of the exemplification of properties. On the one hand, it is argued that property-deity identity is not incoherent when the unique nature of God is taken into consideration. On the other hand, it is claimed that there is nothing incoherent about property-property identity with respect to God.

---

14. The attempt to mitigate the incoherence of saying that God is an abstract object insofar as God is his properties by claiming that God's properties are concrete parts insofar as they are tropes does not succeed. This is because a distinction must still be made between God and his tropes. A trope, a type of concrete object, is a property that is not an instantiated universal, but rather exists in one location at one time and merely has resemblance to other tropes, which explains the ascription of the same general term to more than one trope (Williams, "On the Elements of Being: I"; Williams, "On the Elements of Being: II." See the discussion in Hoffman and Rosenkrantz, *The Divine Attributes*, 59–68.

15. Plantinga, *Does God Have a Nature?*, 57–58.

16. The simplicity doctrine, however, is integral to many classical theological systems.

The Oneness and Simplicity of God

William Mann: God as Property-instance

William Mann defends his interpretation of Aquinas's version of the simplicity doctrine against Plantinga's attack.[17] He addresses two of Plantinga's objections to the state of affairs version of the simplicity doctrine: the identification of God with all of his states of affairs ("Deity-instance identities") and the identification of one state of affairs with another ("instance-instance identities").[18] First, Mann argues that, while it may be true that to assert that God is a property is incoherent, it is not incoherent to claim that God is identical with each of his property-instances, what Mann calls the property-instance view.[19] A property instance is an instantiation of a property. Thus to say that God is a property instance is to say that God is a concrete object and not an abstract object. Moreover, Mann rejects Plantinga's assumption that no property instance is a person.[20] According to him, the absolute distinction between a person as concrete and a property as abstract is invalid insofar as properties may be concrete when they are property instances. He calls into the question the assumption that property instances are ontologically inferior to persons; this is because without its essential properties a person, including God, would not be. Mann then distinguishes what he calls a rich property, which is all the essential and accidental properties of a thing, from other properties. The rich property is a type of all-inclusive super-property. A person is an instance of a rich property, which is that person's complex, conjunctive property consisting of essential and accidental properties. In this way a person is a rich property and a rich property a person. In the case of God, there is one rich property of which God is the concrete instance; this rich property is not complex like those of created persons because it has no accidental properties and because the property instances are identical with one another. Mann writes, "The instance-instance identities, along with the thesis that God has no accidental properties, gives us the result that the rich property associated with God has but one element—*being a Godhead*, which

---

17. Mann, "Divine Simplicity," 456. See also Mann, "Simplicity and Immutability in God."

18. In this work, the former is known as property-deity identity and the later property-property identity.

19. Mann, "Divine Simplicity," 457. Mann argues that Aquinas' version of the doctrine of simplicity is better than Anselm's because Anselm must equate one abstract object with another whereas Aquinas only identifies one of God's attributes with another of God's attributes ("Divine Simplicity," 455).

20. Mann, "Divine Simplicity," 465–68.

is the same property as *being omniscient, being omnipotent,* and all the rest."[21] Mann also rejects the claim that, if he is identified with his rich property-instance, then God is powerless since properties and property-instances are causally inert, having no causal efficacy. Instead, he argues that properties are causal powers and confer those powers on their objects. He writes, "If properties are causal powers and if God is a property, then he is a causal power."[22] In the case of God, there is one causal power corresponding to the one rich property.

Second, Mann addresses the objection to the simplicity doctrine that, if God is identical with his properties instances, then each of his property instances is identical with each of his other property instances. This would mean that every property-instance is the same as every other property-instance, which runs counter to common sense. According to him, in the case of maximally-degreed properties it is possible to assert that properties are identical, even if in non-maximal cases this is not true.[23] He says, for example, of being knowledgeable and powerful: "Yet the two properties converge at their extrinsic maxima; rather they coalesce."[24] Furthermore, he proposes that God's properties be understood by means of the set-extensional view of properties, rather than the predicate synonymy view, so that two divine properties can be co-extensive but still distinct. The latter stipulates that predicate synonymy is necessary for attribute identity. By contrast, according to the set-extensional view, properties are identified with a set of actual objects, which means that the properties identified belong only to the things in the set. In this case, because the identity of a set is determined by its extension, co-extensive properties are identical even though they are non-synonymous.[25] This means that properties that are necessarily co-extensive and co-instantiated are identical without meaning that one divine property is synonymous with all the others. With respect to God, it is not incoherent to say that God's property-instances, or divine

---

21. Ibid., 467.
22. Mann, "Simplicity and Properties: A Reply to Morris," 352.
23. Mann, "Divine Simplicity," 460.
24. Ibid., 461.
25. Ibid., 463. Hughes defends the coherence of what he calls insular properties (*Complex Theory*, 63–67). He writes, "Then any property necessarily had by God and only God will turn out, on the current assumptions, to be God" (66). It would seem, however, that even if one individual alone has a property, one cannot collapse the property and individual into one entity; rather the individual and its property are still conceptually and really distinct.

perfections, to use traditional terminology, all correspond to a single property-instance in God, but without losing the distinctiveness of the multiple property-instances.

Mann proposes that God as a person be understood as the concrete instance of one, causally-effective rich property consisting of convergent maximal properties that are co-extensive and co-instantiated. This proposal provides support for property-deity identity and property-property identity. Mann's defense of the simplicity doctrine, however, gives the impression of being a little desperate. His argumentation relies upon a blunting of the sharpness of linguistic categories.[26] The assertions that properties can be identical without being synonymous when they are necessarily co-extensive and co-instantiated, that maximally-degreed properties are one and the same property, that a rich property is one and many at the same time, that a rich property can be a person and a property and that properties can be both concrete and causal powers seems to amount to conceptual homogenization. It is questionable whether a defense of the simplicity doctrine can rely on this methodology, since almost anything can be proved in the absence of terminological precision. Of particular concern is the confusion of the concepts of exemplification and instantiation.[27] According to Mann, God instantiates his rich property-instance, for which reason God is to be identified with his rich property; his view seems to be that properties are self-instantiating. Conventionally, however, it is held that an individual, as a concrete object, exemplifies a property, whereas an individual's property instantiates it. There is, in other words, a distinction between the individual and its property instance. Thus to identify God with his rich

---

26. Morris, "On God and Mann: A View of Divine Simplicity"; Morris, *Our Idea of God*, 113–18.

27. Wolterstorff, "Divine Simplicity," 138–39. This is contrary to Barry Miller who claims that Mann's view can be defended against Morris by making a distinction between "substantival and adjectival properties" (*A Most Unlikely God*, 75–77). According to him, it is possible to say that an individual is his rich property-instance when the latter is understood to be a substantival property. This would require, however, the identification of a rich-property instance with the individual that exemplifies it, that in which the property is instantiated, and would raise the question of why there is a distinction at all between the two, between subject and substantival predicate. Miller later recognizes that the distinction between God and his rich property-instance, Godhead, a count noun (a noun that can be modified by a numeral), leads to the possibility that the property Godhead could have been exemplified by another God: "The difficulty is that there is no reason why Godhead should not have been instantiated by some God other than the one that did instantiate it" (77). In other words, there is still the distinction, so inimical to the simplicity doctrine, between God and God's rich property-instance.

property-instance is not to play by the usual linguistic rules. It should not be possible to assert that an individual instantiates a property, in particular, a rich property, with the result that it becomes identified with that property. To claim that God is an exception begs the question and removes God from the realm of normal human discourse. In the end, Mann's view that God is identical to his rich property is really nothing other than bare assertion, if it is even meaningful.

In addition, Mann must concede Thomas Morris's objection that identifying God with his property-instance repudiates God's aseity. This is because God becomes dependent on something other than himself, namely his rich property that he instantiates, which is true even if one accepts Mann's view that properties are causal powers.[28] In responding to Morris, Mann's strategy is to identify God's instance of omniscience, for example, with omniscience itself, which God alone has; the same would true for God's other properties. Regardless of whether God alone has a property like omniscience, to identify God with any property, rather than merely his property-instance of it, leaves Mann vulnerable to Plantinga's original criticism that God cannot be a property.[29] Another objection to Mann's defense of the simplicity doctrine is that his assertion that necessarily co-extensive attributes are identical, although not synonymous, appears to be untrue, even on the set-extensional view of properties.[30] On the usual understanding of properties, no one would expect that the amalgamation of maximal properties to become a so-called rich property would result in their becoming identical. How the non-synonymous properties that are one super-property still retain their distinctiveness is not clear. Finally it is pointed out that if God is one rich property-instance, then it is impossible to distinguish between God's necessary and contingent properties, contrary to Mann's claim. Morris writes, "God's properties obviously cannot differ among themselves in modal status if he has in reality only one property."[31]

---

28. Mann, "Simplicity and Properties: A Reply to Morris," 351–52. Gale comments, "There is still the distinction between the multiply instantiatable property of being possessed of such-and-such causal powers and the concrete instantiations of this property; and, thus, the aseity objection is not laid to rest" (*Nature and Existence of God*, 28). See Leftow, "The Roots of Eternity," 195; Miller, *A Most Unlikely God*, 75–77; Vallicella, "Divine Simplicity: A New Defense," 510–12.

29. Vallicella, "Divine Simplicity: A New Defense," 307–8; Gale, *On the Nature and Existence of God*, 27–28.

30. Richards, *The Untamed God*, 222–24; Immink, *Divine Simplicity*, 95.

31. Morris, "On God and Mann: A View of Divine Simplicity," 307.

The Oneness and Simplicity of God

Normally, God's contingent properties are not included as constituting his essence or nature any more than they are for created beings.

Stump and Kretzmann: God's Attributes as Identical in Reference but Different in Sense

Eleonore Stump and Norman Kretzmann disagree with Plantinga that it is impossible to adopt property-property identity without falling into incoherence.[32] They seek to demonstrate that it is not only coherent but that there are theoretical advantages to adopting it. They argue that God's intrinsic properties can be one property because in the case of God a distinction must be made between reference and sense: between God (reference) and the various ways in which God appears (sense). In other words, the simple God has multiple, non-synonymous aspects or manifestations, which human beings know as God's attributes or properties. They write, "What the doctrine requires one to understand about all the designations for the divine attributes is that they are all identical in reference but different in sense, referring in various ways to the one actual entity which is God himself or designating various manifestations of it."[33] The claim is that, in the case of God, perfect F-ness is the same as perfect G-ness, although this is not true in the case of imperfect instantiations of these attributes or properties.[34] Accordingly, the different attributes or properties of God can be considered as "non-synonymous expressions designating quite distinct manifestations of one and the same thing."[35] The fact that the planet Venus is experienced as both the morning star and evening star is said to be an analogue to how the designation of God's attributes or properties are to be understood.[36] This way of understanding God's intrinsic attributes or

---

32. Stump and Kretzmann, "Absolute Simplicity." See Stump, *Aquinas*, 92–130.

33. Stump and Kretzmann, "Absolute Simplicity," 356. See Stump, *Aquinas*, 99–100. Hughes uses the concept of a "supervenience base property" to explain property-property identity, the view that God's properties are identical to one another (*Complex Theory*, 71–87).

34. Hughes, *Complex Theory*, 62.

35. Stump and Kretzmann, "Absolute Simplicity," 356–57.

36. Hughes offers a possible defense for the view that God is his properties based on set theory (*Complex Theory*, 63–67). If properties are identified as the sets of things having the said properties and if only one thing is in a set then the result is that a property is an individual. He calls this a "subsistent property," but prefers the term "insular property." Nevertheless, he rejects this defense because of the problem of shared

properties is also said to be parallel to understanding God's manifestations and effects in time. God as perfect is atemporal and therefore does not do one thing at t1 and something else at t2. Rather, "the atemporal pure actuality that is God can have various manifestations and effects in time."[37]

What Stump and Kretzmann put forward as a defense of property-property identity is a contemporary version of the view, adopted by Aquinas among many others, that a distinction must be made between God's simple nature or essence and his many effects or energies.[38] Such a position, however, is not a *bona fide* defense of the simplicity doctrine, but is a concession that God cannot have true, which is to say, univocal, attributes or properties and be simple at the same time, as Plantinga claims. Their view is that what human beings experience as the divine attributes or properties only appears that way because God cannot have such a multiplicity since he is simple. The use of the example of the morning and evening stars, of course, presupposes that this is indeed analogous to how God has properties, and for that reason has no argumentative value.[39] In fact, it would appear that, in order to preserve the coherence of the simplicity doctrine, Stump and Kretzmann are taking refuge in apophatic theology, to which Plantinga is equally unsympathetic.[40] In addition, as Gale points out that, their view is counterintuitive, because, if anything, one would expect perfect instances of properties to be even more different from imperfect instances of them, rather than converging to one, all-inclusive property.[41] Finally, even if there is an absence of real distinction among God's attributes or properties, as Stump and Kretzmann claim, God would still not be simple because God would be dependent on the one, all-inclusive attribute or property that he exemplifies.[42] The argument, in other words, does nothing to justify property-deity identity.

---

attributes with created things, which precludes the possibility of insular properties (*Complex Theory*, 67–71).

37. Stump and Kretzmann, "Absolute Simplicity," 356.

38. See *SCG* 1.31; *ST* 1.13.4.

39. Vallicella, "Divine Simplicity: A New Defense," 509–10. He writes, "The problem is one of metaphysics, not of the philosophy of language" (510). See Ross, "Comments on 'Absolute Simplicity.'"

40. Sadler holds this view insofar as he rejects realism: that the attributes or properties of God are abstract entities (*Simply Divine: Simplicity as Fundamental to the Nature of God*).

41. Gale, *On the Nature and Existence of God*, 26.

42. Ibid., 25.

The Oneness and Simplicity of God

William Vallicella: Identification of Individual and Property

Seeking to rescue the simplicity doctrine from the charge of incoherence, William Vallicella questions the assumption made by Plantinga that no property, an abstract object, can be an individual, a concrete object.[43] He writes, "The problem arises on the plausible assumption that a categorical chasm divides properties and individuals such that, necessarily, no property is an individual. But this might be an untenable dualism. It might be that some properties are identical to individuals."[44] Vallicella rejects Plantinga's absolute disjunction between the two ontological realms of causally-efficacious, unexemplifiable concreta and causally-inert, exemplifiable abstracta.[45] He first establishes his philosophical terminology. His definition of an individual includes not being multiply exemplifiable and not being exemplifiable by anything distinct from itself, whereas his definition of a property is something that is exemplified.[46] Based on these definitions of property and individual, he claims that it is possible to say that God is a property, as long as God is a property that is not exemplifiable by anything other than himself. This would make a property identical with an individual, in this case God. He concludes, "For if a property Q were exemplifiable only by itself it would count as a property according to (P) but also as an individual according to (I)."[47] He further explains that, if the

---

43. Vallicella, "Divine Simplicity: A New Defense"; Vallicalla "Divine Simplicity."

44. Vallicella, "Divine Simplicity: A New Defense," 512.

45. Vallicella writes, "It is easy to see that Plantinga-style objections will not appear decisive to those who reject his ontological framework. Plantinga, along with many other philosophers, thinks of individuals and properties as belonging to radically disjoint realms despite the fact that individuals exemplify properties. Individuals are causally efficacious concreta whereas properties are casually impotent abstracta. Such an approach to ontology renders the divine simplicity inconceivable from the outset. For if God is a concrete individual and his nature (conceived perhaps as the conjunction of his omni-attributes) is an abstract property, then the general ontology rules out an identity of God with his nature. Any such identity would violate the separateness of the two realms. To identify an unexemplifiable concretum with an exemplifiable abstractum would amount to an ontological category-mistake. At most, a Plantinga-style approach allows for God's exemplification of his nature where the (first-level) exemplification relation, unlike the identity relation, is asymmetrical and irreflexive and so enforces the non-identity of its relata. In short, if God exemplifies his nature, then God is distinct from his nature" ("Divine Simplicity," n.p.).

46. Vallicella defines an individual as follows: "(I) *x* is an individual iff (i) *x* exemplifies properties, (ii) *x* is not multiply exemplifiable, and (iii) *x* is not exemplifiable by anything distinct from itself." Conversely, a property is defined as follows: "(P) *P* is a property iff *P* is possibly such that it is exemplified" ("Divine Simplicity: A New Defense," 512).

47. Vallicella, "Divine Simplicity: A New Defense," 513.

Recent Defense of the Simplicity Doctrine

divine attributes are not multiply-exemplifiable, then each divine attribute is a haecceity, an individual thing. Vallicella is not identifying a property with an individual *simpliciter*, since these are recognizably distinct things: "The property of being a property is distinct from the property of being an individual."[48] Nevertheless, for him a property is identical to an individual in the cases where a property is not multiply-exemplifiable.[49]

In defense of the coherence of the simplicity doctrine, Vallicella makes use of the notion of self-exemplifying properties, such as existence and self-identity (existence *exists* and self-identity is *self-identical*). Such properties are both first-level and second-level properties. Omnipotence, for example, is a first-level property insofar as it is predicated of an object ("God is omnipotent"), but is a second-level property insofar as it is a predicated of itself, a property of a property ("Omnipotence is omnipotent").[50] As already explained, because God's self-exemplifying properties are not multiply exemplifiable, God can be said to be his properties. It follows that in the case of God an individual is identical to a self-exemplifying property. Vallicella uses the example of omniscience: omniscience is self-exemplifying because omniscience is omniscient, but omniscience cannot be separated from the one individual who is omniscient since it is not multiply exemplifiable. The result is that both omniscience is omniscient and God is omniscient, and these are synonymous statements, or, in other words, God is his property. The same can be said of other divine attributes, such as omnipotence. So it turns out that there is nothing incoherent about property-deity identity.

What remains to be proven is that each divine property is identical to the same individual, which is a condition for identifying properties with one another, i.e., property-property identity. Vallicella argues that this would be true if the properties are necessarily co-extensive: given the transitivity of identity it would follow that the properties are identical to one another. He writes, "So one can, without contradiction, hold that there is one individual = God with whom each attribute is identical. And then given the transitivity of identity, it would follow that the attributes are identical with each other."[51] If God is identical to each of his attributes or properties then each of them is identical to all of his other attributes or properties: if God is x and God is y, then x is y. In addition, God's attributes or properties are "modally uniform"

48. Ibid., 514.
49. Ibid., 514.
50. Ibid., 516–17.
51. Ibid., 515.

in the sense that God need only have essential properties and not accidental ones also.[52] It is important to stress that Vallicella's goal is only to establish the possibility that God is identical with his properties or attributes and they with one another against Plantinga's categorical rejection of it.

Vallicella's claim that in the case of God an individual is a self-exemplifying property has the appearance of being forced and contrived. Contrary to what he claims, the distinction between the two ontological realms of causally-efficacious, unexemplifiable concreta and causally-inert, exemplifiable abstracta seems intransigent. It is not an untenable dualism at all, as he claims, but is a presupposition of analytical philosophy and, indeed, of the world of common sense, allowing for no exceptions. Vallicella's definition of an individual as including not being multiply exemplifiable and not being exemplifiable by anything distinct from itself is odd and confusing, since individuals are not exemplified, but rather exemplify properties. Of course, this reworking of the definition of an individual is required to allow him to identify a property with an individual. The suspicion is, therefore, aroused that his argument is circular. Even in the case of a property exemplified by only one individual, the distinction between that property, or abstract object, and the individual, or concrete object, that exemplifies it does not disappear. Vallicella claims only to be seeking to make some room for the simplicity doctrine by proving that an ontological exception is possible: "I would say that the usual definitions, according to which, necessarily, no property is an individual, beg the question against divine simplicity. In so doing they represent an illicit extrapolation beyond what we can claim to know on the basis of the normal range of cases."[53] In other words, it is possible that what is true in things encountered in ordinary experience is not true of God. It would seem, however, that such a conclusion is not possible when the usual definitions of individual and property are accepted and assumed to be applicable to God. In addition, Vallicella's claim that some properties are self-exemplifiable appears sophistical since properties do not exemplify but are exemplified.[54] To claim, for example, that omniscience is omniscient seems to be meaningless. To allow for the possibility of properties being self-exemplifiable conveniently facilitates his identification of God with his properties, since, if a property exemplifies a property and God exclusively exemplifies the same property

---

52. Ibid., 517.

53. Ibid., 513.

54. See Miller, "On 'Divine Simplicity: A New Defense,'" and Vallicella's response in "On Property Self-Exemplification: Rejoinder to Miller."

(i.e., the property is not multiply-exemplifiable), it follows that God is a property. Finally the claim that necessarily co-extensive properties allow for the identification of each property with all the other properties is not convincing. Being necessarily co-extensive does not mean identity if God is not identifiable with his properties.

Brian Leftow: Abstract Object Concretized

In considering the question of whether God is an abstract object, Brian Leftow argues that what he calls the Identity Thesis (that God is identical to his nature, i.e., property-deity identity) does not require the conclusion that God is an abstract object and not a person, as Plantinga claims.[55] He asks why it is that God's identity with his nature means that God is an abstract object and not that God's nature is a person. He writes,

> Plantinga assumes that if God = God's nature, God has all of the attributes usually associated with God's nature and no attributes previously associated with the title "God" which are incompatible with attributes usually associated with God's nature. But why assume this? Plantinga gives no reason. A God who is identical with His nature may have only some abstract-entity features. He may even have none: the claim God = God's nature could inform us that that which is identical with God's nature exemplifies no attributes previously associated with God's nature. So that God = God's nature just does not entail that God has only abstract-entity features, nor therefore that He is abstract.[56]

Leftow asserts that when two things are said to be identical, A = B, then there is one subject of predication. This one thing may have a proper subset of the attributes that A is thought to have and a proper subset of the properties that B is thought to have. As applied to God, if God as person = God's nature, then the one subject of predication, called God, for want of a better third term, may have a subset of the attributes that God as person is thought to have and a subset of attributes that God's nature is thought to have. There is no justification, however, for concluding that God has all attributes associated with God's nature and none associated with God as person. For this reason one cannot conclude that God is an abstract object.

---

55. Brian Leftow reiterates the traditional argument for the simplicity doctrine from God's aseity ("Is God an Abstract Object?," 582–86).

56. Leftow, "Is God an Abstract Object?," 593.

The Oneness and Simplicity of God

Leftow then explains that God as concrete person has "abstract-entity features," because like abstract entities God is likewise omnipresent, timeless and immutable. This does not mean, however, that God is an abstract object.[57] It is just as easily said that an abstract object becomes concretized as it is that God becomes an abstract object.

Taking his cue from Augustine, Leftow claims that Plantinga illegitimately draws the conclusion that if God is identified with his properties, abstract objects, then God is an abstract object and not a person, a concrete object that exemplifies properties.[58] He argues that the opposite conclusion is equally feasible: that the abstract objects are concretized in God as a person and so cease to be abstract. He writes, "But Plantinga takes it without argument that if one identifies God and something abstract, the result is something abstract. It might instead be to eliminate the abstract entity, leaving God as He was."[59] Contrary to some interpreters, Leftow claims that Augustine identifies the Platonic Ideas with God, with the result that the Ideas cease being abstract entities in which God as an individual, a concrete object, participates. He explains,

> Augustine took God as the paradigm replacing all Forms God might have in common with creatures: his "what He has, He is" identifies with Forms God in which God might participate and thereby eliminates the Forms. Say that God is the Good—as Augustine did—and we can adapt the logic just sketched: God's being good is just His being Himself, as the Good's was. The same goes for the rest of the Forms whose place God takes. There is no need for a trope, universal or other abstract constituent to make it true that God is good (etc.): what serves as the standard for all these things does so just by being itself.[60]

The troublesome conclusion that God is an abstraction insofar as God is identified with his properties is avoided by affirming instead that God's properties are concretized as God. The problem now becomes explaining how an abstract object can be a person rather than how a person can be an abstract object.

Plantinga's aim is to demonstrate that incoherence results from the simplicity doctrine, or what Leftow calls the Identity Thesis: on this

---

57. Ibid., 593–94.
58. Leftow, "Divine Simplicity."
59. Ibid., 366–67.
60. Ibid., 370–71.

hypothesis, God a person, a concrete object, becomes a property, an abstract object, which makes no sense. For him, as for most analytical philosophers, the distinction between a property, an abstract object, and the individual that exemplifies, a concrete object, is presuppositional and absolute; the identification of the two is a category mistake, confusing one type of thing for another. Leftow's claim that it is equally feasible to say that an abstract object is concretized in a person as it is to say that a person is an abstract object is irrelevant to Plantinga's argument, since it does nothing to remove the incoherence of the simplicity doctrine. It may be the case that to have God the person as an abstract object or entity is theologically worse than to have an abstract object or entity as God the person. Nevertheless, from the point of view of logical coherence neither is better nor worse. In order to overcome the incoherence of either position, one must resort to special pleading: that God as subsistent existence is the *only* person that is an abstract object or the *only* abstract object that is a person; in so doing, the terms "person" and "property" would be used equivocally, since it is a category mistake to identify a person and a property. In other words, such a theological strategy would require taking refuge in apophatic theology, which Plantinga does not accept.

Nicholas Wolterstorff: Nature as Constituent

Nicholas Wolterstorff argues that modern analytical philosophers misunderstand the traditional simplicity doctrine to mean that God is an abstract object. The reason for this is that medieval philosophers, among whom the simplicity doctrine took shape, worked with a constituent ontology, whereas modern philosophers have adopted a relation ontology. According to the former, a thing *is* a nature (or essence) whereas for the latter a thing *has* a nature (or essence). For a medieval philosopher a thing's nature is "what-it-is-as-such," and is a constituent of it; for this reason, it is "just as concrete as that of which it is a nature."[61] By contrast, for a modern philosopher, a nature is an "abstract entity," as Wolterstorff calls it, which a concrete thing exemplifies as one of its properties; it is a conjunctive property that includes as its conjuncts those properties that an individual has in all possible worlds in which it exists.[62] In other words, a nature as an abstract object is ontologically external to a concrete object and has a relation to it.

61. Wolterstorff, "Divine Simplicity," 141.
62. Ibid., 136, 141.

The Oneness and Simplicity of God

In Wolterstorff's view, when one takes into account medieval constituent ontology, the simplicity doctrine is not incoherent. The assertion that God is simple is the assertion that God is his one constituent, his nature. In other words, it is the denial that God is other constituents that, combined with his nature, would make God an "articulated composite."[63] First, it is denial that God has matter, which would particularize the divine nature. Designated matter (*materia signata*) functions to individuate a nature so that more than one material entity with the same nature can exist at the same time. Second, it is a denial that, unlike every other entity, God has accidents. An accident is not a part of the nature of an individual thing, and for that reason contributes to the compositeness of the thing. Wolterstorff writes,

> Why should there not be a certain entity which, like everything else, just is a certain nature, but which, unlike most or all other entities, is nothing more than that—is not a composite? Such an entity will not be made out of matter. Nor will it have any accidents. It will be just a certain something-as-such, a certain what-it-is-as-such.[64]

On a medieval constituent ontology, the assertion that God is simple is unproblematic because it merely expresses the fact that God is incomposite insofar as he has only one constituent, his nature. The simplicity doctrine only becomes problematic on a modern relation ontology because it must be explained how a concrete object can be identified with an abstract object.

Wolterstorff's claim that medieval theologians used a constitutent ontology rather than a relation ontology, even if true, does not explain how God can be simple.[65] In what he calls relation ontology, a nature is an abstract object, which a concrete object, or what Wolterstorff calls an entity, exemplifies. Even on a constituent ontology, however, a nature is not a concrete object. By medieval theologians Wolterstorff seems to be thinking primarily of Aquinas, since he quotes from Aquinas's *Summa Theologiae*. For Aquinas there is a difference between a nature and the suppositum to which it belongs, even in the case of a concrete object or entity that is immaterial and without accidents. This is because a nature is not a concrete object, which explains why in the case of material things matter is identi-

---

63. Ibid., 141.
64. Ibid., 142.
65. There was no consensus among medieval theologians on the question the ontological status of essences or natures. See Rogers, "The Traditional Doctrine of Divine Simplicity," 165 n. 2.

fied as that which individuates a form. Thus, even on a constituent ontology, it is still the case that an immaterial concrete object without accidents, such as God, would be distinguished from and depend upon its nature as its only constituent. There must be, therefore, another reason to draw the conclusion that God is simple, which for Aquinas is that God as first cause requires that he depend on nothing in order to be what he is, i.e., first cause. This for him explains why God alone is perfectly simple. Such a conclusion, however, scandalously violates the basic ontological distinction between a nature (or essence) and its suppositum, which both medieval and modern philosophers adopt as fundamental to all philosophical discourse, despite differences in vocabulary.

Barry Miller: God as Limit Case

Analytical philosopher Barry Miller argues that, contrary to Plantinga's claim, the simplicity doctrine is coherent. His rather inaccessible argument depends upon the distinction between a limit case and a limit simpliciter. The latter describes the upper limit of a graded series of exemplifications of a property that is still a member of the series. All members of the series, including the limit simpliciter, are ordered according to graded variations in a defining characteristic. The limit case, however, is "that in which a defining characteristic of the members has been varied to the point of extinction."[66] It does not belong to the series; rather there is an absolute difference between it and members of the series. For this reason, the limit case functions as an alienans adjective, an adjective that is used in order to change the sense of the noun that it qualifies. If, as Miller claims, God's perfect properties are limit cases (which is the same thing as saying that God is the limit case), then there is no univocity between them and their imperfect counterparts. For example, God's power is not the limit simpliciter of a graded series of instances of powers, from which it follows that God is not to be thought of as the most powerful of all beings, a perfect being. Rather God's perfect power is the limit case of power, which means that it is not an instance of power at all. Nevertheless, as the limit case of power, God's perfect power is not completely unrelated to instances of imperfect power. God's perfect properties as limit cases can be used to explain the apparent incoherence of the simplicity

---

66. Miller, *A Most Unlikely God*, 9.

doctrine, i.e., property-deity identity and property-property identity: God as simple makes sense in terms of limit case but not limit simpliciter.

Miller then moves to a consideration of God as subsistent existence, which is a barely recognizable version of Aquinas's view of the same. Contrary to the analytical philosophical tradition, he conceives existence as that which receives a bound and is thereby individuated; as a bound of existence, the individuator is then actualized. In other words, existence is understood as a type of substratum upon which a bound is imposed. A bound to existence is to be distinguished from its instance of existence; an entity as individuator is logically prior to existence with respect to individuation, but is logically posterior to existence with respect to actuality. Miller refers to God as a zero-bound instance of existence. He means that God is the limit case bound of existence, or an entity that does not require a bound to be individuated and actualized, unlike every other entity. The term "bound" is being used in an alienated sense, for a zero-bound instance of existence is not bounded at all: God is neither individuated nor an instance of existence by means of a bound. Miller then explains that the limit case bound of existence is the same as the limit case instance of existence: they have an identical referent, God. The limit case bound of existence is an entity that does not require a bound to be individuated, and this is God; the limit case instance of existence is an entity that does not require a bound to be actualized, and this is God also. According to Miller, this is what God's subsistent existence means. He writes, "The notion of Subsistent Existence, then, is the notion of the entity which is jointly and identically the limit case instance of existence and the limit case bound of existence."[67] In the case of God considered as zero-bound instance of existence, the distinction between individuation and actualization is eliminated. Expressed in more traditional terms, God's existence (*esse*) is his essence (*essentia*), insofar as God's existence is not limited, or contracted, by an essence, but contains actually every possible perfection.[68] Miller also explains that there is no incompleteness in subsistent existence insofar as it lacks an individuator, a bound to existence, and insofar as it, not being an individuator, lacks an instance of existence and so is a bound that has nothing to bound.

---

67. Ibid., 67.

68. This is not true of entities other than God because their essence is not existence. An instance of existence is logically posterior to its existence in respect of actuality, but logically prior with respect to individuation.

Recent Defense of the Simplicity Doctrine

Presupposing the validity of his defense of the notion of subsistent existence, Miller argues that it is coherent to hold that God's perfect, or subsistent, properties are such that they are identical to God and to one another, just as the simplicity doctrine claims. For him, the implication of God as subsistent existence is God's simplicity. In his view, contrary to that of many philosophers, existence is not the thinnest possible attribute but rather is the richest; existence's richness is then bounded and contracted by an individuator.[69] What is not incomplete with respect to existence is subsistent existence, from which it follows that subsistent existence is identical to its properties and the properties to one another. Whatever properties belong to subsistent existence must likewise be zero-bounding, in which case they are identical to unbounded existence and therefore to one another. In limit cases, properties are not incomplete with respect to existence, by which is meant that the properties are not the properties that they are in non-limit cases since in the latter they are bounded and so are one thing and not another. Likewise, if they were instances of existence they would not be zero-bounding. The lack of incompleteness, or bounds, means that no distinctions can be made between subsistent existence and its properties and among the properties themselves. Because God is subsistent existence, God's limit-case properties are not properties at all in the sense that they are distinct from one another and from God. If subsistent existence could be distinguished from its properties and the properties from one another then subsistent existence and its properties would not be zero-bounded. In so arguing, Miller seems to be appealing to the principle of the identity of indiscernibles.[70]

Miller's defense of the coherence of the simplicity doctrine is dependent on the validity of the applicability of the concept of limit cases to God and his view of subsistent existence. Furthermore, his view of subsistent existence depends upon his interpretation of existence as the only real property that does not inhere in the individual, but is individuated by being bound by an individuator.[71] This view is certainly idiosyncratic among analytical philosophers and may be dismissed by some as no better than poetic expression. Even if one accepts these assumptions, however, it would still seem that Miller is actually agreeing with Plantinga that property-deity

---

69. Miller, *A Most Unlikely God*, 37–44.

70. If, for every property F, object x has F if and only if object y has F, then x is identical to y.

71. Miller, *A Most Unlikely God*, 33–35.

identity and property-property are incoherent *unless* God is understood as a zero-bound instance of existence. His defense of the simplicity doctrine amounts to nothing more than saying, contrary to perfect-being theology, that God is an extraordinary object of discourse: God does not have true properties, that predication with respect to God is equivocal since God's properties are zero-bounding. In fact, despite Miller's protestations, it is arguable that that God is not an object of discourse at all. In other words, Miller's view is a restatement of the traditional view that the essence or nature of God is unknowable, but using terminology derived from analytical philosophy. His position assumes that God, unlike all other entities, is not an individual and an instance of existence and so the normal rules of discourse do not apply to him. The incoherent statements associated with the simplicity doctrine in fact could be interpreted as expressions of the unknowability of God. As already indicated, Plantinga is not sympathetic with taking refuge in the ineffability of God as a defense of the simplicity doctrine, viewing it as a theological dodge.[72] Besides, if he is truly unknowable insofar as he is a zero-bound instance of existence then God cannot even be said to be simple, unless the term simple signifies the negation of all bounded existence, or created being.

Conclusion

What these attempts to defend the coherence of the simplicity doctrine have in common is that God is made to be a valid exception with respect to the exemplification of properties. First, it is argued that property-deity identity is not incoherent given the unique nature of God. Such an undertaking, however, is doomed to failure from the beginning, since the distinction between a concrete object or individual and an abstract object or property is presuppositional and so intractable. It is axiomatic that an abstract object or property be distinguishable from a concrete object or individual that exemplifies it. So, as Plantinga demonstrates, once one consents in some way or another to think about God as having properties, then God cannot be said to be simple. If one persists in asserting that God as subsistent existence, unlike created beings, is identical with his properties, then God necessarily becomes so exceptional that he can no longer be an object of ordinary discourse, since predicate terms expressing properties when used of God are not being used univocally. In this case, there is actually

---

72. Plantinga, *Does God Have a Nature?*, 10–26.

agreement with Plantinga's conclusions: God cannot be simple and have true properties. The incoherence of property-deity identification remains true even when the difference between God and his properties is attenuated by distinguishing a property-instance from a property and God's many properties are collapsed into one rich property. The other philosophical devices used to defend property-deity identity against the accusation of incoherence tend to be either so contrived as to be incredible or are irrelevant. Second, attempts to justify property-property identity with respect to God are likewise unconvincing. It is again presuppositional that one property is not the same as another. Even if properties are co-extensive, one property is not the same as another property or all the other properties. The claim that property-property identity is the consequence of *perfect* instantiation of properties or that God's properties are zero-bound or limit-case properties is actually a concession that God does not have true properties, but has properties only in an equivocal sense.

Approach Two: Truthmaker Account of Divine Simplicity

As a technical term, "truthmaker" originates among contemporary philosophers who use it to denote that which entails the truth of certain statements or predications. This concept is brought to bear on the debate about divine simplicity. The truthmaker account seeks to overcome Plantinga's criticism of the simplicity doctrine as incoherent. By appealing to the notion of a truthmaker, the modest goal of such theorists is to demonstrate that to think of God as simple is at least coherent. Its advocates agree that property-deity identity leads to the absurdity of asserting that the concrete object or individual known as God is identical to one or more abstract objects or exemplifiable properties.[73] Instead of appealing to properties as the entities that cause God's essential predicates, however, the truthmaker account appeals to God, a concrete object or individual, as their cause. The result is that God is identical to the truthmaker of his essential predications, such as being omniscient or omnipotent, which is to say that God is identical to God. The nominalizations of the divine predications, such as omniscience or omnipotence, refer not to properties but to their truthmaker, which is God, or, put in traditional terms, God is his attributes. To say that God is

---

73. Brower, "Making Sense of Divine Simplicity"; Brower, "Simplicity and Aseity"; Bergmann and Brower, "A Theistic Argument against Platonism"; Dolezal, *God without Parts*, 154–63.

the truthmaker of his essential predications denies that there is a plurality of constituents or properties that make up God; it is rather to affirm that God himself is what makes God what God is.

The truthmaker account of divine simplicity is anticipated by Graham Oppy.[74] He rejects the conclusion that, since God shares properties with human beings, God cannot be simple since he cannot be identical to his properties. Rather he considers the possibility that one could identify two things as having the same predicate without assuming that they do so for the same reason, namely that both have the same property insofar as they exemplify the same universal. Oppy assumes a possible discontinuity between the grammatical structure of sentences and the nature of the reality that makes true sentences true. In other words, it is not necessarily the case that a predicate corresponds to a property or that grammatically-identical, true sentences are true for the same reason. He writes, "Suppose that it is not the case that every predicate that features in true atomic sentences expresses a property. Suppose, more generally, that the nature of the reality that makes true sentences true does not have the same structure that is reflected in the grammatical structure of the sentences that are made true."[75] In his view, the presupposition that universals apply both to God and created things requires scrutiny: "I think that we need to suppose that there are no predicates *that express universals* that apply to God and to other entities."[76] The reasons that a created thing is F and God is F is not the result of the same truthmaker having the same metaphysical structure, namely the exemplification of the same universal: "The metaphysically fundamental categories that somehow combine to make these sentences true are heterogeneous."[77] In some cases, human language is deceptive by grammatically allowing the predicate F to be applied to God and a created thing when God is F for one reason and the created thing is F for quite another. The common syntactical structure of the sentences is no certain guide to the metaphysical structure of the truthmakers for each sentence.[78] For this reason it is possible to affirm that God is F and a created thing x is F without

---

74. Oppy, "The Devlish Complexities of Divine Simplicity."
75. Ibid., 15.
76. Ibid., 16.
77. Ibid., 16.
78. Oppy writes, "We are already committed to the view that the surface syntax of true sentences is no decent guide to the metaphysical structure of the truthmakers for those sentences" (ibid., 20).

being committed to the position that God and x both have the property F. It is not that to predicate F of a created thing and of God is equivocation or merely analogical, since both are genuinely F; rather it is to deny that there is one property that is being expressed by the predicate F in its occurrences in the two propositions. He writes, "That two sentences of the form 'a is red' and 'b is red' are both true does not entail that there is some universal that plays a role in making both of these sentences true."[79] Oppy accepts the traditional view that God has no properties and agrees that the neo-Platonic intuition about God is correct. He prefers to adopt a position of skepticism about "the ontological category to which God belongs."[80]

Jeffrey E. Brower and Michael Bergmann provide a full exposition of the truthmaker account of the simplicity doctrine. They explain that by truthmaker is meant, not efficient causality, but logical necessitation.[81] Brower writes,

> Despite the misleading connotations suggested by its name, the notion of a truthmaker is not to be understood in terms of (efficient) causality. On the contrary, it is to be understood in terms of broadly logical necessitation—as is evident from the fact that contemporary philosophers habitually speak of truthmakers as *entailing* the truth of certain statements or predications.[82]

A truthmaker is what explains the truth of something, necessitates the truth of the predication that it makes true, or that in virtue of which something is the case.[83] A concrete object or individual cannot be the truthmaker of its contingent, extrinsic predications; these require abstract objects or properties as constituents of the concrete object or individual.[84] Brower, however, proposes to think of God as identical to the truthmakers of the predications made of him, rather than God's properties, as is

---

79. Ibid., 15.

80. Ibid., 19.

81. Bergmann and Brower, "A Theistic Argument against Platonism"; Brower, "Making Sense of Divine Simplicity"; Brower, "Simplicity and Aseity"; Nash-Marshall, "God, Simplicity, and the *Consolatio Philosophiae*."

82. Brower, "Making Sense of Divine Simplicity," 17.

83. Brower, "Simplicity and Aseity," 110–11; Bergmann and Brower, "A Theistic Argument against Platonism," 23.

84. Brower, "Making Sense of Divine Simplicity," 19–20; Brower, "Simplicity and Aseity," 111–12.

The Oneness and Simplicity of God

traditionally done.[85] The rejected view that all predication should be understood in terms of exemplifiable properties conceived as abstract universals has its roots in Platonism and is endorsed by contemporary analytical theists.[86] The concept of truthmaker is metaphysically or ontologically neutral, in the sense that no commitment is taken with respect to the nature of the truthmaker.[87] To adopt the concept of the truthmaker as the explanation of the truth of a predicate allows for the possibility that this entity is either an exemplifiable property, an abstract object, or an individual, a concrete object, such as God.

Divine simplicity follows from the truthmaker account of divine predication since there is one truthmaker for all essential predications of God, God himself. Brower writes, "On this interpretation, therefore, divine simplicity just amounts to the claim that God is the truthmaker for each of his true intrinsic predications."[88] Bergmann and Brower explain that there is nothing untoward about asserting that "God is identical with the *referents of abstract singular terms* corresponding to each of the true intrinsic predications that can be made about him."[89] Each abstract nominalization, such as goodness, power, wisdom, corresponding to a predication of God, such as good, powerful and wise, has a referent. Contrary to the defenders of Platonism, including analytical philosophers, the referent of each abstract nominalization is not an exemplifiable property but God himself. In other words, God is the truthmaker for each predication of God. It follows that God is his own goodness, power and wisdom, which is what the simplicity doctrine asserts. In responding to possible objections to his truthmaker account of divine simplicity, Brower clarifies that there is no reason that one thing, in

---

85. Brower, "Making Sense of Divine Simplicity," 19. In a footnote he adds that God is the *minimal* truthmaker for each of his true predications; the intention of this qualification is to eliminate the possibility that part of an entity could also be a truthmaker of a predication about the entity. He writes, "God is the *minimal* truthmaker for each of his true intrinsic predications—where an entity E is a minimal truthmaker for a predication P just in case E is such that no proper part of it also makes P true.... [T]his qualification is needed since on some theories of truthmaking, if E is a truthmaker of P, then so is anything of which E is a part. Once this qualification is added, however, the absolute simplicity of God follows immediately. For if God had any proper parts, there would be true intrinsic divine predications (namely, about these parts) whose minimal truthmakers would not be God (but the parts) (Brower, "Simplicity and Aseity," 125 n. 23).

86. Bergmann and Brower, "A Theistic Argument against Platonism."

87. Ibid., 25–26; Brower, "Making Sense of Divine Simplicity," 15.

88. Brower, "Simplicity and Aseity," 112.

89. Bergmann and Brower, "A Theistic Argument against Platonism," 30.

particular, the simple God, cannot be the truthmaker for many, conceptually-distinct predications.[90] This is because truthmakers allegedly do not stand in a one-to-one correspondence with the predications that they make true.

James Dolezal defends his own version of the truthmaker account of the simplicity doctrine.[91] He explains, "The notion of 'truthmaker' fulfills the function that properties play in the various Property Accounts of the DDS [doctrine of divine simplicity] without importing any of the problems that properties pose for a simple God."[92] He questions the viability of the property-deity account of divine simplicity insofar as it is "the nature of a property *qua* property to exist by dependence upon a substance."[93] In Aristotelian fashion, Dolezal stresses the ontological primacy of concrete objects or individuals, what he calls a substance, and the dependence on them of abstract objects or properties, which are exemplifiable by them. The category error common to both detractors and defenders of the property account of the simplicity doctrine, however, is holding that perfections attributed to God can *only* be caused by corresponding properties that God possesses.[94] Instead Dolezal argues that divine attributes refer not to properties but to "the divine substance itself."[95] God is the truthmaker of all that is predicated of God, not God's properties. This is not true of created things, for what is attributed to them refers to properties. He concludes,

> But substances and properties cannot be in a single ontological category. Therefore, when an attribute is ascribed to God its referent is the divine substance, while, when applied to a creature, the same attribute refers to a property in the creature. Both the divine nature and the creaturely properties function as truthmakers for their respective attributes. It follows, then, that not all predications are made true by the same underlying ontological structure.[96]

In other words, God himself is that by which he is what he is, not his properties.[97]

---

90. Brower, "Simplicity and Aseity," 115–17.
91. Dolezal, *God without Parts*, 154–63.
92. Ibid., 155.
93. Ibid., 155.
94. Ibid., 159.
95. Ibid., 160.
96. Ibid., 160.
97. Ibid., 162.

The truthmaker account of divine simplicity is not a legitimate response to Plantinga's criticism of the simplicity doctrine because it is nothing more than the bare assertion that God as simple can inexplicably have properties without having properties. In truthmaker theory every true proposition has a minimal truthmaker, i.e., a smallest portion of reality, that makes the proposition true. What this means is that each true proposition has only *one* truthmaker, which is not the truthmaker of other true propositions. The nature of the truthmaking relation is such that each true proposition is made true by virtue of a relation to one existent reality.[98] It would seem, therefore, that to claim that a simple God can function as a truthmaker for many non-existential, true propositions is a misuse of truthmaker theory. Because of God's simplicity, the possibility of a miminal truthmaker for each of God's attributes is ruled out. The option that remains is the incoherent view that God is the one and only truthmaker for all true propositions about him. In other words, it leads to the meaningless assertion that God is the cause of God's being God. The incoherence can be eliminated, or at least attenuated, by claiming that God does not have true attributes or properties, but that is to take refuge in divine ineffability since it is axiomatic that a concrete object or individual like God have essential properties that identify him as what he is. It could also be countered that there is no incoherence if anything with essential predicates can be considered simple insofar as it is self-identical, and so can be the truthmaker of all its essential predications. If God is simple in this sense, however, then God's simplicity is not unique and is even trivial.

Approach Three: Modification of Simplicity Doctrine

Another proposed defense of the simplicity doctrine is to modify it in order remove its incoherent elements, while retaining what is considered to be its true intention. Advocates of this solution propose that the simplicity doctrine may be affirmed using the traditional terminology, but only after its offensive elements are pared away, both property-deity identity and property-property identity. Typical of this approach, Swinburne writes, "However, those who claimed that God is identical with his properties were, I think, trying to say something very important and quite probably true, even if they did not express it very well and it is now time to bring out what it is."[99] Generally,

---

98. Schmitt, "The Deadlock of Absolute Divine Simplicity."
99. Swinburne, *The Christian God*, 163.

it is held that the divine attributes are indeed co-extensive, but this should not be taken to mean that they are identical with one another or that God is identical with his properties. Thus Plantinga's critique functions as a catalyst to overhaul and rework the simplicity doctrine.[100]

Although incomposite and simple are synonyms for most advocates of the simplicity doctrine, Robert Burns proposes that God can be both incomposite in the sense of not having *separable* parts and complex in the sense of having more than one *inseparable* part. In other words, rejecting composition in God does not require accepting divine simplicity, so long as being composite is primarily understood as being liable to decomposition.[101] He proposes that Aquinas equivocates when he equates being incomposite and simple because the opposite of simple is complex, not composite. This obviates the need to hold that God is simple in the sense of being identical with his attributes and therefore allows the possibility that God is both incomposite and complex. He writes, "Unquestionably, a single first cause would have to possess unassailable integrity but it does not follow that it might not be characterized by an internal set of factors which might be distinguishable from one another, given their eternally secure harmony."[102] It follows that it is possible for God not to be composed of separable parts (because of God's "eternally secure harmony"), but still be complex. Burns holds that there is a correspondence between human predication with reference to God and the essence of God: the multiple predicates correspond to several factors in the divine essence. Rejecting Aquinas's position that it is impossible to predicate anything univocally of God, he explains, "But if *within* the divine essence there were a plurality of interdependent factors, then in principle they would be distinguishable from one another, for which purpose the multiplicity of terms in human language might not be the disadvantage which Thomas argues it must be."[103]

Richard Swinburne also re-evaluates the traditional formulation of the simplicity doctrine and removes what he considers to be its offensive and unnecessary elements. Committed to upholding the view that there is

---

100. Long before Alvin Plantinga, Charles Hodge rejects the traditional view found among "schoolmen" and Protestant scholastics that God's attributes are identical to one another and only differ in name on the grounds that it leads to a destruction of the knowledge of God (*Systematic Theology* 1.371–72). He is an exception, however, representing an anti-speculative, common sense approach to theology.

101. Burns, "The Divine Simplicity in St. Thomas."

102. Ibid., 273.

103. Ibid.

"a natural unity to the divine nature,"[104] he embraces the simplicity doctrine, but not in its patristic and medieval expressions, which leads ultimately to the identity of divine properties with one another and with God (property-property identity and property-deity identity).[105] He appreciates Mann's more nuanced property-instance proposal based on Aquinas' version of the simplicity doctrine, namely that "the instances of the divine properties in God are the same as each other and as God," but still finds that it is inadequate to provide a basis for the simplicity doctrine.[106] He explains Aquinas' view as the result of "residual Platonism" with the result that God's property-instances are considered as abstract objects that function as ontologically-prior parts of God unless they are identified with God. He writes, "All of this becomes unnecessary once we abandon Platonism and acknowledge that abstract entities are not constituents of the universe but mere convenient fictions."[107] Swinburne does not explain, however, how abstract objects or properties and concrete objects or individuals, what he refers to as substances, relate to each other, such that the former are not ontologically prior or independent but are merely "convenient fictions." It might seem that he is adopting a nominalist position, were it not for his own explanation of the unity of divine nature. He claims that the unity of divine properties should be grounded in one property: "The unity of the divine properties follow from their being included in a simple property, which I have called having pure, limitless, intentional power."[108] Unfortunately, he does not clarify how the many divine properties are manifestation of this one property; it appears, in fact, that he is creating *ad hoc* philosophical framework and terminology to justify accepting the simplicity doctrine in this modified form.

Likewise prompted by Plantinga's critique of it, Gerrit Immink seeks to salvage what he considers to be the true intention of the simplicity doctrine, which he thinks Plantinga has not fully appreciated. That true intention is to express God's aseity and otherness.[109] The simplicity doctrine asserts that God has all his perfecting properties essentially.[110] In other

---

104. Swinburne, *The Christian God*, 160.
105. Ibid., 160–63.
106. Ibid., 161.
107. Ibid., 162.
108. Ibid., 162.
109. Immink, *Divine Simplicity*, 34–35.
110. Ibid., 172–78.

words, God has multiple perfections, or properties, but these are united in an inextricable way, "the essential *unity* or *union* between God and his perfecting properties."[111] It follows that God can be said to be equivalent to his essential properties, but without implying that God is identical to his properties or that each property is one and the same as every other property. What Immink calls the "identity thesis" serves to emphasize the unity between God and his perfecting properties, but this should not be taken so far as to adopt the property-property identity view: "However we must not defend this unity in such a strong sense that it results in a strict identity between all God's perfecting properties. All we need to say on this point is that God has his divine properties *essentially*."[112] He criticizes Aquinas and other overly-zealous advocates of the simplicity doctrine for exceeding proper theological limits.[113] He writes, "Aquinas did conclude that they are identical in God, but this conclusion is not required by the theological notion of God's unity. It is a consequence of Aquinas' overaccentuation of God's otherness."[114] A corollary to this version of the simplicity doctrine is that God is immutable, indestructible and everlasting.[115]

John Frame holds that, in spite of the numerous arguments advanced in favor of the simplicity doctrine, some complexity in God should not be ruled out.[116] Contrary to the denials of its advocates, he alleges that the doctrine of the Trinity precludes adopting the simplicity doctrine.[117] He explains that the inclination to reject multiplicity in God is actually an influence of the neo-Platonic view of God as absolutely one. In Frame's view, what the simplicity doctrine is really seeking to express is "God's necessary existence."[118] In addition, he claims that, since God relates to us as a person not as attributes, another purpose of the simplicity doctrine is to remind us that God is personal: "It is a biblical way of reminding us that God's relationship with us is fully personal."[119] When Scripture describes God, for example, as spirit, light, and love, the intention, according to Frame,

111. Ibid., 175.
112. IIbid., 176.
113. See Oliphint, *Reasons for Faith*, 91–95.
114. Immink, *Divine Simplicity*, 176.
115. See Miller, *A Most Unlikely God*, 93–94.
116. Frame, *The Doctrine of God*, 225–30.
117. Ibid., 227–28.
118. Ibid., 228.
119. Ibid., 230.

The Oneness and Simplicity of God

is to describe God's essence. He means that human predication of God is univocal in the sense that each predicate has a corresponding attribute or property in God.[120] It follows that God's attributes or properties are not synonymous but are "genuine complexities in his essence," although God's unity must also be seen in the divine complexity.[121]

Finally, developing Duns Scotus's notion of formal distinction, Yann Schmitt substitutes "absolute indivisibility," what he calls moderate simplicity, for absolute simplicity, which is to say property-property identity, a complete lack of complexity.[122] In his view, God is a multiplicity, but the divine properties inseparably belong to one subject, God.

To remove property-deity identity and property-property identity from the simplicity doctrine is actually to reject it and substitute for it what Dolezal calls the Harmony Account.[123] What remains is not the simplicity doctrine as traditionally articulated but rather the unity of God, the necessary co-extension of divine attributes or the indestructibility of God.[124] In each case, it is so pared down that it no longer warrants being called divine simplicity. Rather than modify the simplicity doctrine so radically, it would be better no longer to refer to God as simple. Furthermore, the theological problem still remains of how God the indivisible substratum can depend upon his necessary and co-extensive properties without thereby denying his aseity and sovereignty, which Plantinga identifies as the intuition behind the simplicity doctrine.

Approach Four: Simplicity as Negative Theology

Taking their theological cue from Thomas Aquinas, some theologians have argued that Plantinga's critique of the simplicity doctrine misses the mark because he assumes that it is intended to affirm something about God, when, in fact, its true intention is to deny something about God.[125] To think that the purpose of the simplicity doctrine is to describe God in Parmenidean fashion as a homogenous, indivisible, eternal, immutable, one-of-a-kind entity misses the point completely. Rather, interpreted nega-

120. Ibid., 228; see 208–9.
121. Ibid., 229.
122. Schmitt, "The Deadlock of Absolute Divine Simplicity."
123. Dolezal, *God without Parts*, 136–44.
124. See ibid., 143–44; Miller, *A Most Unlikely God*, 94.
125. See the earlier work: Ward, *The Concept of God*, 157–58.

tively, God's simplicity functions to express God's otherness: to assert that God is simple, or, better, incomposite, is to deny that God is anything like created things. In other words, God is other than all concrete objects in human experience, which are all composite in nature, and has none of the other properties that are corollaries to being composite, such as mutability, finitude, corruptibility, contingency and so forth. In fact, the incoherence of the simplicity doctrine that Plantinga exposes may even be interpreted as commending it an expression of the otherness of God.

David Burrell interprets Aquinas's version of the simplicity doctrine apophatically, holding that the affirmation that God is simple is the denial that God is like created things (he prefers to use the term simpleness).[126] He writes, "Simpleness does not name a characteristic of God. . . . It is a shorthand term for saying that God lacks composition of any kind. And that bit of metaphysical jargon is itself a shorthand way of remarking that no articulated form of expression can succeed in stating anything about God."[127] According to him, to say that God is simple is to say that God is incomprehensible and ineffable. He explains further that simplicity is a formal feature of divinity and so is not a property in the usual sense of the word.[128] He writes, "Formal features concern our manner of locating the subject for characterization, and hence belong to a stage prior to considering attributes as such."[129] The simplicity doctrine serves to guarantee that, when speaking about God, one is speaking about the one who, not having a genus, does not belong to the world but is the beginning and end of all things.[130] Burrell explains, "So the formal feature of divine simpleness is intended to distinguish God from everything else—God's creation. That is, divine simplicity assures God's distinction from 'all things' as well as

---

126. Burrell, *Aquinas, God and Action*, 12–19; Burrell, *Knowing the Unknowable God*, 46–47; Burrell, "Distinguishing God from the World," 3–19.

127. Burrell, *Aquinas, God and Action*, 18.

128. Burrell, "Distinguishing God from the World," 5–10.

129. He suggests that simplicity along with eternity could be called *ur*-properties if one insists on using the term property of God (Burrell, "Distinguishing God from the World," 5).

130. Richards is sympathetic to the interpretation of the simplicity doctrine as an instance of negative theology (*The Untamed God*, 215–16). Although not in Scripture, simplicity is said to be an extension of the holiness of God. Likewise, Keith Ward holds that simplicity (and infinity) functions to deny that "concepts which apply to finite, separated realities are applicable to God" (*The Concept of God*, 158).

The Oneness and Simplicity of God

providing the ground for asserting the gratuity of creation."[131] Furthermore, God as simple is none other than his own existence.

Brian Davies likewise suggests that the key to understand the simplicity doctrine is to interpret it as negative or apophatic theology. Its purpose is not to assert in which mode God has his properties but to deny that God has them at all; it is not a description of God, but a statement about what God is not.[132] He explains further that the simplicity doctrine is an exercise in logical grammar. He writes,

> To cast things in a more modern idiom, the Thomist doctrine of divine simplicity is an exercise in "logical grammar"; its aim is to tell us the sort of conclusions about God which are not to be drawn. And one thing being said by it is that God is not to be thought of (cannot be known) as something with properties distinguishable from each other, or as something we can conceive of as distinct from the nature we ascribe to it.[133]

Rather than being a positive statement about the nature of God, the simplicity doctrine, that God "is divinity through and through without parts or aspects," is a denial that God has a nature in any sense intelligible to human beings and so is the affirmation that God is incomprehensible.[134] A further implication of the simplicity doctrine includes that God is not a created thing, but creator *ex nihilo*, from which it follows that, unlike created things, God has no body, no genus/species and potentiality. In addition, it denies that God is an individual, since to be an individual requires being distinguishable from other individuals of the same kind.[135]

Lawrence Dewan calls into question the validity of Plantinga's dismissal of Aquinas's version of the simplicity doctrine because of the naïvete of its "metaphysical anthropomorphism."[136] In other words, Plantinga assumes that notions such as being and goodness are "fundamentally homogenized or univocal," so that their meanings are limited to the mode that they have in human experience, an imperfect mode.[137] Although he

---

131. Burrell, "Distinguishing God from the World," 6–7.

132. Brian Davies, "Classical Theism and the Doctrine of Divine Simplicity," 58–59; Davies, "A Modern Defence of Divine Simplicity."

133. Davies, "A Modern Defence of Divine Simplicity," 555.

134. Ibid., 549.

135. Ibid., 556–58.

136. Dewan, "Saint Thomas, Alvin Plantinga, and the Divine Simplicity," 151.

137. Ibid., 150–51.

does not say so explicitly, Dewan seems to hold that to assert that God is simple is really to deny that God is like any created being. He explains that Plantinga's mistake is to assume that God and created things both *exemplify* properties. He writes,

> A word like "property," insofar as it includes *inherence* in its signification, and not merely in its mode of signifying, could never be properly said of God. . . . To attempt, as Plantinga does, to apply "property" (which to Plantinga himself clearly conveys *inherence*: otherwise it would cause no difficulty) to creatures and to God suggests he has failed to grasp to doctrine of analogy between creatures and God.[138]

In Dewan's estimation, Plantinga mistakenly assumes that God and created things share in common the fact that properties inhere in both as individuals, that they have the same mode of being. This line of reasoning leads to the conclusion that God is a property insofar as God is simple. The error is to assume that properties inhere in God in the same way that they inhere in finite, created things, rather than subsisting in God (in the Thomistic sense). For this reason, he rejects Plantinga's "possible world" approach, typical of analytical philosophy, according to which, if he exists at all, God is a part of a possible world and is subject to necessary truths in all possible worlds. Dewan's view is that God cannot be considered to be a being among other beings in possible worlds, but is beyond all possible worlds. He writes, "In Thomas Aquinas' metaphysical approach, to prove the existence and expose the nature of God is to take the mind *beyond* any and every possible world to its source."[139] According to him, what is said of beings in a possible world as inhering in them exist in God in a higher mode: "Perfections which exist in a possible world pre-exist in God in a higher mode."[140] This higher mode is subsistence, which implies simplicity. Furthermore, Plantinga fails to appreciate fully Aquinas's teaching about analogy, that properties cannot be attributed univocally to created things and to God, because what exists imperfectly as properties inhering in creatures is only analogous to God's subsistent perfections. Unlike Plantinga, Aquinas holds that, based on experience of sensible, material things, human reason by analogy, using "discernible laws of being," can arrive at the conceptual construction of a highest cause, "in which being is neces-

138. Ibid., 144–45.
139. Ibid., 151.
140. Ibid., 151.

sarily found in a new *simplicity*."[141] What exists in an imperfect mode in composite, created beings exists in a perfect mode in the simple first cause. Terms that are used to signify the imperfect mode cannot be used of the perfect mode: "Words like 'property' and 'accident' are designed to signify the *imperfect modes themselves*."[142] Contrary to Plantinga, he holds that the analogical nature of the knowledge of God explains the apparent incoherence of the simplicity doctrine.

To interpret the simplicity doctrine as a piece of negative or apophatic theology is not to do justice to the clear intention underlying its many historical formulations. While it is true to say that God as simple is other than all created things, it is not the case that God's simplicity is merely the negation of createdness. The negation of being created is being uncreated or ingenerate, not being simple. In other words, the purpose of asserting that God is simple is not solely to deny the possibility of univocal predication of God. Rather, even though there may be some confusion in some articulations of it, the simplicity doctrine is intended to characterize positively the mode of God's existence in contrast to that of created things. For some philosophers and theologians, God as simple does indeed mean that he should indeed be understood in a Parmenidean fashion as a homogenous, indivisible, eternal, immutable, one-of-a-kind entity. In fact, it is somewhat misleading to say that God is simple, a positive term, rather than incomposite, a negative term, if the meaning of such a statement is that God is not like any created thing. Besides, if the simplicity doctrine is synonymous with the otherness of God, then it is a redundant, since there are many others terms used for this purpose.

Using Aquinas as inspiration and support for the interpretation of the simplicity doctrine as negative or apophatic theology is problematic because Aquinas himself is not methodologically consistent. He claims that, since God's essence is unknowable, whatever is asserted about God can only be an expression of what God is not. Divine simplicity is said to be the denial of compositeness in God (*ST* 1.3). Yet almost immediately after outlining this apophatic theological methodology, Aquinas inconsistently makes positive statements about the mode of divine being based upon the negation of various aspects of the compositeness of created being: the negations have positive correlates. Thus, in spite of his claim that divine simplicity is an expression of what God is not, in particular the denial that there is any

---

141. Ibid., 150.
142. Ibid., 144.

Recent Defense of the Simplicity Doctrine

composition in God, Aquinas, to whom the interpreters of the simplicity doctrine as negative theology appeal, also understands simplicity positively as a description of the divine mode of being. For example, the conclusion that God as simple is his own essence or nature is clearly not merely a negation, in spite of the fact that its meaning is not fully comprehensible to human intelligence (*ST* 1.3.3). Likewise, his conclusion that God as simple is form itself (*ipsa forma*) or being itself (*ipsum esse*) describes the divine mode of being and is not merely theological negation (*ST* 1.3.7).[143] Those who claim that God's simplicity functions negatively as a means of expressing God's otherness than created beings repeat Aquinas's error by slipping into interpreting the simplicity doctrine positively as a description of the divine mode of being when they claim, for example, that God as simple means that God is subsistent existence.

---

143. Only Aquinas's denial that God is in a genus is a negation that has no positive correlate (*ST* 1.3.5).

5

Concluding Summary and Evaluation

THE SIMPLICITY DOCTRINE ENTERS Christian theology from Greek philosophy, which in itself does not automatically disqualify it on the assumption that it is an unwarranted intrusion into the purity of biblical teaching. Nevertheless, after a consideration of all the evidence, the conclusion that there is no basis for ascribing simplicity to God seems inescapable. The rejection of the simplicity doctrine means that Christian theologians are not saddled with making sense of its two unusual implications: property-deity identity and property-property identity. The arguments from Scripture used in support of the simplicity doctrine are weak to the point of being unconvincing, which is not surprising given the doctrine's nonbiblical origin. Clearly the alleged scriptural support is *post factum* justification of a pre-existing belief. Likewise the claim that divine simplicity is explicative of the concept of God is also unsuccessful for various reasons. Scripture teaches that YHWH alone is God and that the other gods are not truly God. Without the questionable presupposition that simplicity is ontologically superior to compositeness, to move from the confession of the numerical oneness of God to the confession of divine simplicity is without warrant. Modern defenses and reiterations of the simplicity doctrine also fall well short of establishing it as a positive assertion about the nature of God; there is obviously no advantage to reformulating it using analytical philosophical categories, since to do so does not make it more convincing. It is one thing to confess that there is one God, but quite another to know the essence or nature of this one God, if indeed one can even ascribe an

Concluding Summary and Evaluation

essence or nature to God. Rather it seems prudent to resist the admittedly natural impulse to affirm more about God than is allowable.

Among modern defenders of the simplicity doctrine there are some who suggest that it is defensible as long as it is understood as negative theology: that God as simple means no more than God is other than all created things. If this is what it means, however, the simplicity doctrine is redundant because there are other theological concepts that perform that function, in particular God's ingenerateness, or even the biblical concept of holiness. The disadvantage of using simplicity to express the otherness of God is that it so easily becomes a positive assertion about God, in accordance with the inveterate human tendency to exceed the limits of human knowledge. Besides, this is not what the majority of advocates of the simplicity doctrine intend, not even those who claim that it is negative theology. Rather, its advocates do indeed intend it as a description of the divine mode of being.

It might be thought that the rejection of the simplicity doctrine means that by default God must be composite: one could argue apagogically that if one member of a disjunctive pair is rejected then the other is affirmed. It is a false inference, however, that God must be composite if God is not simple because a third option is possible. That third option is to reject the disjunction entirely: God is *neither simple nor composite*. What both sides of the debate have in common is the assumption that God is a substance who has attributes, or to use more modern terminology, a concrete object, i.e., individual, that exemplifies properties, which are abstract objects. The dispute is over how or in which mode God has attributes or exemplifies properties. All agree that, since he is incorporeal, God could have only metaphysical attributes or properties. On the one hand, proponents of the simplicity doctrine argue in the case of the substance or concrete object known as God first that there can be no distinction between God and any one of God's attributes or properties and second that each attribute or property is the same as all the others. In this way, God is delineated as a unique substance or concrete object insofar as only God is simple. On the other hand, the doctrine's detractors contend that such statements are incoherent, and argue that God as a substance or concrete object could only be composite, like every other substance or concrete object, although in a unique and superlative manner as the greatest conceivable or maximally great being. Morris, for example, holds that God must be thought of as having parts, although the parts are dependent on God and not

The Oneness and Simplicity of God

vice versa.[1] Perhaps though the presupposition that God is a substance that has attributes or a concrete individual that exemplifies properties should be called into question. For this reason, rejecting the simplicity doctrine does not *ipso facto* mean that one is committed to the theological model of God as composite.

Scripture's stress on the otherness of God subverts the hypothesis that God should be conceived as a possible object of human experience and understanding. In the Hebrew Bible, holiness is predicated of God in order to express God's separateness from all things, or God's otherness. Holiness is that in virtue of which God is God and different from what is not God.[2] For this reason, God is said to be incomparable with respect to human beings and the other gods.[3] Despite their differences, what all created things have in common is that they are substances with attributes or concrete objects that exemplify properties. One could therefore argue that God's otherness requires that God not be conceived as a substance with attributes or a concrete object exemplifying properties in any sense, even as simple. In other words, substance is not a concept that describes the mode of existence of whatever can be characterized as existing in itself (*per se ens*), including God; rather God is excluded even from this category.[4] Thus one must reject the univocism implicit in understanding God as the greatest conceivable or maximally great being, as perfect-being theologians do. John Locke notes that human beings generally conceive God as a substance, one consisting of simple ideas derived from reflection, such as existence, duration, knowledge, power, pleasure, happiness and so forth (*Ess.* 2:23:36–38).[5] The difference between God as substance and other substances is that the simple ideas that are compounded to make the complex idea of God are infinite.[6] Locke insightfully recognizes, however, that to conceive of God

---

1. Morris, "God and the World: A Look at Process Theology," 136. See Moreland and Craig, *Philosophical Foundations for a Christian Worldview*, 524.

2. See Smith, *The Indescribable God*, chap. 1.

3. For example, it is said in the Song at the Red Sea, "Who is like you among the gods, O Yahweh" (Exod 15:11) and Isaiah asks, "To whom then will you liken God, or what likeness will you compare with him?" (Isa 40:18–19).

4. See Aquinas, *De ver.* 1.1.

5. For John Locke, substance is a type of complex idea originating as an inference of the necessity of a substratum underlying a collection of ideas that occur together, a "support of such qualities which are capable of producing simple ideas in us; which qualities are commonly called accidents" (*Ess.* 2.23.2).

6. Each of these simple ideas, insofar as it admits of degrees, is multiplied without

Concluding Summary and Evaluation

as a substance in this way is misleading. He writes, "For, though in his own essence . . . God be simple and uncompounded; yet I think I may say we have no other idea of him, but a complex one of existence, knowledge, power, happiness, &c., infinite and eternal" (*Ess.* 2.23.36). According to Locke, the reason that the depiction of God as a substance is misleading is because God is simple. Why Locke thinks that, unlike a created substance, God can only be simple is never explained.[7] Rather than affirming that, because he is simple, God must not be thought of as a substratum, not even one with infinite attributes, it would have been more consistent with Scripture's stress on the otherness of God if Locke had affirmed that what God is in himself is unknown to human beings, a position for which Kant even more insightfully argues subsequently.

According to Kant, the category of substance, which includes subsistence and inherence, is limited in its application to phenomena in space and time, and cannot be extended beyond the realm of possible experience; the result of doing so is always transcendental illusion. In the first analogy of experience, Kant explains what he means by the "principle of the permanence of substance"[8]: "In all variation by appearances, substance is permanent, and its quantum in nature is neither increased nor decreased" (*PR* A182/B224).[9] Substance is the experience of the same thing at different times; such things have a permanence and objectivity that perceptions do not have.[10] Although time cannot be perceived, substance represents time in general by being that to which all change and co-existence relates (*PR* A182/B225).[11] Substance is the substrate of all that is real; whatever is

---

end.

7. To assert that God is "simple and uncompounded" seems to run counter to Locke's empiricism. Locke may hold that the simplicity doctrine is revealed in Scripture, which he considers to be divine revelation.

8. Grundsatz der Beharrlichkeit der Substanz.

9. Dei allem Wechsel der Ercheinungen beharrt die Substanz, und das Quantum der selben wird in der Natur weder vermehrt noch vermindert.

10. The category of substance in its most general sense is explained as "the concept of something that can exist as a subject but never as a mere predicate" (der Begriff einer Subsanz, d. i. von etwas, das als Subject, niemals aber als blosses Prädicat existiren könne) (*PR* B149). The schema of substance is that of "permanence of the real in time, that is, the representation of the real as a substrate of empirical determination of time in general, and so as abiding while all else changes" (ist die Beharrlichkeit des Realen in der Zeit, d. i. die Vorstellung desselben al seines Substratum der empirischen Zeitbestimmung überhaupt, welches also belibt indem alles Andere wechselt) (*PR* A144/B183).

11. See Strawson, *The Bounds of Sense: An Essay on Kant's Critique of Pure Reason*,

The Oneness and Simplicity of God

affirmed is of substance. Kant writes, "All that belongs to existence can be thought only as a determination of substance."[12] In other words, human experience invariably is of permanent substrata, to which accidents, or properties, are assigned and in which they are believed to inhere (*PR* A188–89/B231–32).[13] This is consistent with and required of the Newtonian physics of Kant's day but, as many philosophers have pointed out, it is also true of the world of common sense.[14] Kant then explains that to ask whether God, the transcendental ground of all experience, is a substance is meaningless because the categories that are being used to describe God have only empirical employment, being applicable only to objects of possible experience (*PR* A696–97; B724–25).[15] To think of God as a substance is a mistake, albeit a common and understandable one. Likewise, in his discussion of the physico-theological proof, Kant outlines how, in order to explain the unity of contingencies in experience, all possible perfections are uncritically and illegitimately combined into a single substance as the self-sufficient cause of the order of the whole (*PR* A623; B651).[16] Kant's conclusion that God cannot be conceived as a substance is consistent with Scripture's emphasis on the otherness of God. When transcending the empirical and speaking about God, the theologian has no option but to represent God as a substance having accidents, or properties, for otherwise no discourse would be

---

128–30.

12. Die Substanz, an welcher alles, was zum Dasein gehört, nur als Bestimmung kann gedacht werden (A182/B225)

13. See *PR* A678–79; B706–707.

14. According Thomas Reid, it is a first metaphysical principle of common sense that qualities inhere in a subject—either body or mind.

15. Kant explains that theologians uncritically argue that the primordial being must be simple, since it would be improper to say that what presupposes it constitutes its parts, since this would give ontological priority to the parts: "We cannot say that a primordial being consists of a number of derivative beings, for since the latter presuppose the former they cannot themselves constitute it. The idea of the primordial being must therefore be thought as simple" (*PR* A579/B607). Likewise, the derivation of all things from this primordial being cannot be understood as its division, for this implies that it is merely an aggregate. Kant says, "On the contrary, the supreme reality must condition the possibility of all things as their ground, not as their sum" (*PR* A579/B607). The error, however, in objectifying the transcendental ideal is to create an object of which experience is impossible, for the understanding never has the totality in view. This means that the idea of God so defined above has no empirical employment and therefore is meaningless.

16. Although respectful of it, Kant rejects the physico-theological argument because it presupposes the cosmological argument, which he discredits because it depends on the ontological argument.

Concluding Summary and Evaluation

possible. Nevertheless, contrary to Plantinga's assessment,[17] it must always be kept in mind that to understand God as a substance, or a concrete object, i.e., an individual, is to make use of what Kaufman calls "the available referent" rather than "the real referent," since God is other than all objects of human experience.[18] The only valid theological option is to desist from thinking of God in terms such as subsistence and inherence, of parts belonging to a whole, except in an accommodated way. In other words, it is to reject a naïve Aristotelianism, according to which God cannot be unless he is a substance (ὑποκείμενον or οὐσία).[19]

It follows that merely to ask whether God as a substance or concrete object is simple or composite is methodologically disallowed. Even on the assumption that it is unitive and meaningful, the concept of a metaphysical part is not applicable to God, in which case it is meaningless to assert that God is simple or composite. To undertake an investigation into the nature of God as a substance or a concrete object is to enter into transcendental illusion, to use Kantian terminology. To think of God in terms of substance with attributes or concrete object with properties, even as a superlatively great being, could be described as refined anthropomorphism. God is only a quasi-substance, or analogically a concrete object. To use a crass comparison, to ask whether God is simple or composite is like inquiring into the size of God's feet after reading that God walked in the garden (Gen 3:8). For this reason, Plantinga's argument that God cannot be simple because God is a person, a type of concrete object, is misguided. The question of whether God in himself is either composite or simple ought to be set aside, in spite of the natural urge to answer it one way or another. It cannot be affirmed either that God has properties or is his properties. Likewise, God's properties are neither distinct from and nor identical to one another. To affirm or deny any of these two disjunctive options is to make a theological pseudo-proposition.

In contradistinction to advocates of perfect being theology, those who hold the simplicity doctrine are to be commended for seeking to preserve God's otherness, which is expressed by affirming that God, unlike all created things, is his attributes or properties and everything else that this is believed to entail.[20] The intention to preserve divine otherness, however,

---

17. Plantinga, *Does God Have a Nature?*, 10–26.
18. Kaufman, *God the Problem*, 85.
19. Contrary to Hoffman and Rosenkrantz, *The Divine Attributes*, 59–68.
20. James Dolezal identifies the common element in objections to simplicity doctrine

does not extend far enough because proponents of the simplicity doctrine still assume that God is a substance or concrete object, albeit a unique one insofar as only God is simple. The affirmation that God is simple functions as a way of differentiating the divine mode of being from its opposite, being an implication of the nature of God as unchangeable or as first principle. The unfortunate result is that God is often depicted naively in a Parmenidean fashion as a homogenous, indivisible, eternal, immutable, one-of-a-kind entity. The error in this is the assumption that it is possible to determine the divine mode at all, even by means of taking negations and objectifying them in order to make positive affirmations. Augustine, for example, recognizes the inappropriateness of understanding God as a substance in the Aristotelian sense; for this reason God cannot be said to have any of Aristotle's nine types of predicates outlined in his *Categories* (*Conf.* 4.16.28–29). Rather than being content to deny that God is a substance, however, Augustine erroneously affirms the simplicity of God as God's unique mode of being. It would be better to say that God is neither composite nor simple, because God is beyond all human conceptuality.

It is preferable to adopt an apophatic theological methodology, according to which, as already explained, a distinction is made between how God is experienced by human beings and how God is in himself. Whatever is said about God is really only an expression of how God appears to created beings, as opposed to a description of the divine mode of being. This is more consistent with the biblical position that God is identifiable as God from what he does: "For you are great and do wondrous deeds; you alone are God" (Ps 86:10). The intention of apophatic theology is to preserve the otherness of God by making no positive affirmations about God in himself. Such a view is often expressed by affirming that the nature or essence of God is unknowable to created beings, even though God reveals himself in various, accommodated ways to his creation.[21] The use of apophatic theological method has a long and fruitful history in Christian theology. Interpreting Jer 23:23–24 "I am the God who draws near," Clement of Alexandra distinguishes between the unknowable essence of God and the knowable power of God. He claims that, although he "is in essence remote"

---

as univocism, the assumption that God is a being who differs from other beings by degrees (*God without Parts*, 29–30). His view is that the denial of the simplicity doctrine leads to the denial of God's absoluteness, the rejection of the idea of a "single ontological continuum" to which God and created things belong. See Sokolowski, *The God of Faith and Reason*, 41–52.

21. See Smith, *The Indescribable God*, chap. 2.

Concluding Summary and Evaluation

(πόρρω μὲν κατ' οὐσίαν), God is the one who draws near in power (δύναμις) (*Strom.* 2.2). By power he means what God does. For Clement, it is axiomatic that human beings can never comprehend what God *is*, the essence of God: "For how is it that what is begotten can have approached the unbegotten" (τὸ ἀγέννητον) (2.2). God as unbegotten is absolutely unlike what is begotten, even to the point of not being conceivable as a substance with an essence. Nevertheless, human beings constantly experience the power of God in the sense of the creative and sustaining effects of God. He writes, "For the power of God is always present, in contact with us" (2.2). These effects become for created beings the attributes of God, by which God is known. Similarly, Origen asserts that "God is unknowable and inestimable," which are synonymous expressions, each referring to God's incomprehensibility. The reason that God is incomprehensible is said to be that God's "nature (*natura*) cannot be grasped or seen by the power of any human understanding" (*Prin.* 1.1.5). Similarly, Origen makes a distinction between the nature of God and the "works of divine providence" (*opera divinae providentiae*), or God's effects in creation. Whereas the former cannot be known, the latter can be known and used to formulate an inadequate idea of God, a pragmatic substitute for the unknown nature. He compares God to the sun, upon which human beings cannot look, and God's works to the rays of the sun at which human eyes can look (*Prin.* 1.1.6). He even states his agreement with Celsus who favorably quotes Plato's *Timaeus* to the effect that it is difficult to know God and even more difficult to make God known (*Tim.* 28c) (*Con. Cels.* 7.42). Finally, according to Gregory of Nyssa, while the essence of God is inaccessible, the energies of God, what God does, are not. He writes, "For God is not an expression, neither has he his essence in voice or utterance.... But he is named ... not what he is essentially ... but he receives his appellations from what are believed to be his energies in regard to our life" (*Con. Eunom.* 2.1.149). The attributes predicated of God do not express God's *essence* but rather God's *energies* as experienced by human beings. This point he makes succinctly by saying that "essence is prior to energies" (προϋγέστηκε τῶν ἐνεργειῶν ἡ οὐσία) (*Con. Eunom.* 2.1.150). He re-applies the expression in Phil 4:7 "which passes all understanding," originally ascribed to God's peace, to the divine essence (*Con. Eunom.* 2.1.154).

Now it is sometimes true that, in order to express the unknowability of God, apophatic theologians argue that, because he is simple, God can have no real predicates and what can have no predicates cannot be known

The Oneness and Simplicity of God

as anything. From this it follows that any statement about God cannot be accepted as literally or univocally true. They contrast God's *apparent* multiplicity and knowability with God's *actual* simplicity and unknowability. John Chrysostom, for example, interprets John 1:18 "No one has ever seen God" to mean that "No one knows God in his essence with complete exactness" (*De incomp.* 4.22). He contrasts several statements in Scripture in which it is stated that someone has seen God (Isa 6:1; Dan 7:9; 1 Kgs 22:19; Amos 9:1) with John 1:18 (*De incomp.* 4.17–19). He reconciles Scripture with itself by asserting that what people saw was not the essence of God, but God's condescensions to human limitations; he thereby gives hermeneutical priority to John 1:18. He explains that, since "God is simple" (ἁπλοῦς), being "not composed of parts" (ἀσύνθετος) and therefore "without figure and form" (ἀσχημάτιστος), it follows that no one could have seen the essence of God in the sense of coming to know what God is. What is simple cannot have predicates, and so cannot be said to be anything. So for Chrysostom divine simplicity functions as a means of expressing the unknowability of God, since what is simple cannot but be unknowable.[22] The problem with this theological approach is that simplicity is still a predicate, and functions for most advocates of the simplicity doctrine as a descrip-

---

22. Basil understands God's simplicity to imply God's incomprehensibility. He writes, "God alone is called a monad and unity because it is God's nature to be simple, which makes him incomprehensible (ἡ δὲ μονὰς καὶ ἑνὰς τῆς ἁπλῆς καὶ ἀπεριλήπτου οὐσίας ἐστι᾽ σημαντική)" (*Ep.* 8). In his view, for God to be simple is to be completely other than any created being, and so incomprehensible. Hilary likewise holds that God as simple is incomprehensible: "God is a simple Being: we must understand him by devotion, and confess him by reverence. He is to be worshipped, not pursued by our senses, for a conditioned and weak nature cannot grasp with the guesses of its imagination the mystery of an infinite and omnipotent nature (quia natura moderata et infirmis naturae infinitae et potentis sacramentum intelligentiae opinione non occupet). In God is no variability, no parts, as of a composite divinity (non est itaque diversus compositae divinitatis partibus), that in him will should follow inaction, speech silence, or work rest, or that he should not will, without passing from some other mental state to volition, or speak, without breaking the silence with his voice, or act, without going forth to labor. He is not subject to the laws of nature, for nature has received its law from him: He never suffers weakness or change when he acts, for his power is boundless, as the Lord said, Father, all things are possible for you (Mark 14:36)" (*De Trin.* 9.72). Finally, Maximus Confessor connects God's superessentiality with God's simplicity. He seems to argue that God cannot be an essence, by which is meant to have an essence, because a distinction would be made between God as a thinker and God's essence as an object of thought. But God's simplicity precludes positing such a duality between thinker and thought. He writes, "He is entirely above essence and entirely above thought, since he is an invisible monad, simple and without parts" (*Cent. gnost.* 1.82).

tion of the divine mode of being. In other words, the idea that God is a substance or concrete object is retained, except that God's mode of being, unlike that of all created things, is to be simple and not composite. To affirm that what makes God other than all created things and unknowable is his simplicity, however, seems inconsistent, if the goal is to establish the complete unknowability of God in himself; this is because simplicity is still a predicate, functioning as a positive statement about the divine mode of being. God may be unknowable because he is simple but in one respect, at least, he is still knowable: as simple. It would be better to contrast the unknowable God with God as experienced and interpreted by created beings. The former is neither a simple substance nor a composite one, but inaccessible to human beings, whereas the latter is a composite substance with various attributes, or a concrete object exemplifying properties. Adopting this approach precludes the possibility of asking the question of how or in what mode God as a substance or individual has attributes or exemplifies properties, the answering of which then becomes a theological pseudo-proposition, including that God does so as simple.

Bibliography

Allen, Leslie C. *Jeremiah: A Commentary*. The Old Testament Library. Louisville: Westminster John Knox, 2008.
Anatolius, Khalid. *Athanasius*. London: Routledge, 2004.
Andersen, F. I. *The Hebrew Verbless Clause in the Pentateuch*. Journal of Biblical Literature Monograph Series 14. Nashville: Abingdon, 1970.
Babbitt, Frank C. *Plutarch. Moralia V*. Loeb Classical Library 306. London: Heinemann, 1936.
Barnard, Leslie W. *Justin Martyr: His Life and Thought*. Cambridge: Cambridge University Press, 1967.
Bavinck, Herman. *Reformed Dogmatics*, vol. 2, *God and Creation*. Grand Rapids: Baker, 2004.
Bennett, Daniel. "The Divine Simplicity." *Journal of Philosophy* 66 (1969) 628-37.
Bergmann, Michael, and Jeffrey Brower. "A Theistic Argument against Platonism (and in Support of Truthmakers and Divine Simplicity)." In *Oxford Studies in Metaphysics*, vol. 2, edited by Dean W. Zimmerman, 357-86. Oxford: Clarendon, 2006.
Binder, Stéphanie E. *Tertullian, On Idolatry and Mishnah Abodah Zarah*. Jewish and Christian Perspectives 22. Leiden: Brill, 2012.
Binger, Tilde. *Asherah: Goddesses in Ugarit, Israel and the Old Testament*. Journal for the Study of the Old Testament Supplement Series 232. Sheffield, UK: Sheffield Academic, 1997.
Blakeney, Edward H., editor. *Lactantius' Epitome of the Divine Institutes*. London: SPCK, 1950.
Block, Daniel I. "How Many is God? An Investigation into the Meaning of Deuteronomy 6:4-5." *Journal of the Evangelical Theological Society* 47 (2004) 193-212.
Borchardt, C. F. A. *Hilary of Poitiers' Role in the Arian Struggle*. The Hague: Nijhoff, 1966.
Borgen, Peder. *Philo of Alexandria. An Exegete for his Time*. Supplements to Novum Testamentum 86. Leiden: Brill, 1997.
Brower, Jeffrey. "Making Sense of Divine Simplicity." *Faith and Philosophy* 25 (2008) 3-30.
———. "Simplicity and Aseity." In *The Oxford Handbook of Philosophical Theology*, edited by Thomas P. Flint and Michael C. Rea, 105-28. Oxford: Oxford University Press, 2009.
Bruggemann, Walter. *A Commentary on Jeremiah: Exile and Homecoming*. Grand Rapids: Eerdmans, 1998.
Brunner, Emil. *The Christian Doctrine of God*. Philadelphia: Westminster, 1949.

Bibliography

Burns, Peter. "The Status and Function of Divine Simpleness in *Summa Theologiae* Ia, qq. 2–13." *Thomist* 57 (1993) 1–26.

Burns, Robert M. "The Divine Simplicity in St. Thomas." *Religious Studies* 25 (1989) 271–93.

Burrell, David B. *Aquinas, God and Action*. London: Routledge and Kegan, 1979.

———. "Distinguishing God from the World." In *Faith and Freedom: An Interfaith Perspective*. Oxford: Blackwell, 2004.

———. *Knowing the Unknowable God*. Notre Dame: University of Notre Dame Press, 1986.

Calabi, Francesca. *God's Acting, Man's Acting: Tradition and Philosophy in Philo of Alexandria*. Leiden: Brill, 2008.

Carabine, Deidre. *The Unknown God*. Louvain Theological and Pastoral Monographs 19. Grand Rapids: Eerdmans, 1995.

Chappell, V. "Aristotle's Conception of Matter." *Journal of Philosophy* 70 (1973) 679–96.

Charnock, Stephen. *The Complete Works of Stephen Charnock*, vol. 1, *Discourses on Divine Providence and The Existence and Attributes of God*. Edinburgh: Nichol, 1864.

Childs, Brevard. *The Book of Exodus*. The Old Testament Library. Louisville: Westminster John Knox, 1974.

Clark, Mary T. "De Trinitate." In *The Cambridge Companion to Augustine*, edited by Eleonore Stump and Norman Kretzmann, 91–102. Cambridge: Cambridge University Press, 2001.

Clarke, Samuel. *A Discourse concerning the Being and Attributes of God*. London: Botham, 1732.

Clements, Ronald E. *Old Testament Theology*. Atlanta: John Knox, 1978.

Cogan, Mordecai, and Hayim Tadmor. *II Kings*. Anchor Bible 11. New York: Doubleday, 1988.

Cooper, John W. *Panentheism. The Other God of the Philosophers*. Grand Rapids: Baker, 2006.

Corrigan, Kevin. *Reading Plotinus: A Practical Introduction to Neoplatonism*. West Lafayette, IN: Purdue University Press, 2005.

Craigie, Peter C. *The Book of Deuteronomy*. The New International Commentary on the Old Testament. Grand Rapids: Eerdmans, 1976.

Cross, Richard. *Duns Scotus on God*. Aldershot, UK: Ashgate, 2005.

Dancy, R. M. *Two Studies in the Early Academy*. SUNY Series in Ancient Greek Philosophy. Albany, NY: State University of New York Press, 1991.

Davids, Peter. *Commentary on James*. New International Greek Testament Commentary. Grand Rapids: Eerdmans, 1982.

Davies, Brian. "Classical Theism and the Doctrine of Divine Simplicity." In *Language, Meaning and God*, edited by Brian Davies, 51–74. London: Chapman, 1987.

———. "A Modern Defence of Divine Simplicity." In *Philosophy of Religion: A Guide and Anthology*, edited by Brian Davies, 549–64. Oxford: Oxford University Press, 2000.

Delling, Gerhard. "MONOS QEOS." *Theologische Literaturzeitung* 77 (1952) 469–76.

Dever, William G. *Did God Have a Wife? Archaeology and Folk Religion in Ancient Israel*. Grand Rapids: Eerdmans, 2005.

Dewan, Lawrence. "Saint Thomas, Alvin Plantinga, and the Divine Simplicity." *The Modern Schoolman* 66 (1989) 141–51.

Dillon, John. *Alcinous. The Handbook of Platonism*. Oxford: Oxford University Press, 1996.

———. *The Middle Platonists*. Rev. ed. Ithaca, NY: Cornell University Press 1996.

Dodds, Eric R. "The Parmenides of Plato and the Origin of the Neoplatonic 'One.'" *The Classical Quarterly* 22 (1928) 129–42.
Dolezal, James E. *God without Parts: Divine Simplicity and the Metaphysics of God's Absoluteness*. Eugene, OR: Pickwick, 2011.
Dorner, Isaak. *System der Christlichen Glaubenslehre*, vol. 1, *Grundlegung oder Apologetik*. Berlin: Hertz, 1879.
Driver, Samuel H. *Deuteronomy*. The International Critical Commentary. Edinburgh: T. & T. Clark, 1902.
Dunn, Geoffrey D. *Tertullian*. London: Routledge, 2004.
Dunn, James D. G. *Romans 9–16*. Word Biblical Commentary 38b. Dallas: Word, 1988.
Dupont, Jacques. "MONWI SOFWI QEWI (Rom 16:27)." *Ephemerides Theologicae Lovanienses* 22 (1946) 362–75.
Fee, Gordon D. *The First Epistle to the Corinthians*. The New International Commentary on the New Testament. Grand Rapids: Eerdmans, 1987.
Feinberg, John. *No One Like Him: The Doctrine of God*. Wheaton, IL: Crossway, 2001.
Finley, Thomas J. *Joel, Amos, Obadiah: An Exegetical Commentary*. Chicago: Moody, 2003.
Frame, John M. *The Doctrine of God*. Philipsburg, NJ: Presbyterian & Reformed, 2002.
Franks, Christopher A. "The Simplicity of the Living God: Aquinas, Barth, and Some Philosophers." *Modern Theology* 21 (2005) 275–300.
Freedman, David Noel. "YHWH of Samaria and His Asherah." *Biblical Archaeologist* 50 (1987) 241–49.
Frick, Peter. *Divine Providence in Philo of Alexandria*. Texts and Studies in Ancient Judaism 77. Tübingen: Mohr-Siebeck, 1999.
Fung, Ronald Y. K. *The Epistle to the Galatians*. The New International Commentary on the New Testament. Grand Rapids: Eerdmans, 1988.
Gale, Richard. *On the Nature and Existence of God*. New York: Cambridge University Press, 1991.
Garland, David E. *1 Corinthians*. Baker Exegetical Commentary on the New Testament. Grand Rapids: Baker Academic, 2003.
Garrigou-Lagrange, Reginald. *God, His Existence and Nature*, vol. 2, *A Thomistic Solution to Certain Agnostic Antinomies*. St. Louis: Herder, 1936.
Gerson, Lloyd P. *Plotinus*. London: Routledge, 1994.
Gilson, Etienne. *Being and Some Philosophers*. 2nd ed. Toronto: Pontifical Institute of Medieval Studies, 1952.
Goldingay, John. *Message of Isaiah: A Literary-Theological Commentary*. London: T. & T. Clark, 2005.
Grant, Robert M. *Gods and the One God*. Philadelphia: Westminster, 1986.
———. *Irenaeus of Lyons*. London: Routledge, 1997.
Green, Gene L. *Jude and 2 Peter*. Baker Exegetical Commentary on the New Testament. Grand Rapids: Baker, 2008.
Guthrie, Kenneth S. *Numenius of Apamea: The Father of Neo-Platonism*. London: Bell and Sons, 1917.
Gwynn, David. *Anthanasius of Alexandria: Bishop, Theologian, Ascetic, Father*. Oxford: Oxford University Press, 2012.
Hägg, Henny Fiskå. *Clement of Alexandria and the Beginnings of Christian Apophaticism*. Oxford Early Christian Studies. Oxford: Oxford University Press, 2006.
Hadley, Judith N. *The Cult of Asherah in Ancient Israel and Judah: Evidence for a Hebrew Goddess*. Cambridge: Cambridge University Press, 2000.

Bibliography

Hall, Gary H. *Deuteronomy*. Joplin, MO: College, 2000.
Hampton, Stephen. *Anti-Arminians*. Oxford: Oxford University Press, 2008.
Hanson, Paul D. *Isaiah 40–66*. International Bible Commentaries Series. Louisville: Westminster/John Knox, 1995.
Harrington, Daniel. *1 Corinthians*. Sacra Pagina 7. Collegeville, MN: Liturgical, 1999.
Heppe, Heinrich. *Reformed Dogmatics*. Grand Rapids: Baker, 1978.
Hines, Brian. *Return to the One*. Bloomington, IN: Unlimited, 2004.
Hobbs, T. R. *2 Kings*. Word Biblical Commentary 13. Waco, TX: Word, 1985.
Hodge, Charles. *Systematic Theology*. 3 vols. Grand Rapids: Eerdmans, 1977.
Hoffman, Joshua, and Gary S. Rosenkrantz. *The Divine Attributes*. Oxford: Blackwell, 2002.
Holloway, Maurice R. *An Introduction to Natural Theology*. New York: Appleton-Century-Crofts, 1959.
Holmes, Stephen R. "'Something Much Too Plain to Say': Towards a Defense of the Doctrine of Divine Simplicity." *Neue Zeitschrift für Systematische Theologie und Religionsphilosophie* 43 (2001) 137–54.
Horsley, Richard A. *1 Corinthians*. Abingdon New Testament Commentaries. Nashville: Abingdon, 1998.
Hough, Lynn H. *Athanasius: The Hero*. Cincinnati: Jennings and Graham, 1906.
Hughes, Christopher. *On a Complex Theory of a Simple God*. Ithaca, NY: Cornell University Press, 1989.
Hughes, Gerard J. *The Nature of God: An Introduction to the Philosophy of Religion*. London: Routledge 1995.
Hunt, Emily J. *Christianity in the 2nd Century: The Case of Tatian*. London: Routledge, 2003.
Immink, F. G. *Divine Simplicity*. Kampen: Kok, 1987.
Kaufman, Gordon. *God the Problem*. Cambridge: Harvard University Press, 1972.
———. *Systematic Theology: A Historicist Perspective*. New York: Scribner's Sons, 1978.
Kelly, J. N. D. *Early Christian Doctrines*. 5th rev. ed. London: Continuum, 2000.
Kenny, Anthony. *Aquinas*. New York: Hill and Wang, 1980.
———. *The Five Ways: St. Thomas Aquinas' Proofs of God's Existence*. London: Routledge, 1969.
Klein, George L. *Zechariah*. New American Commentary 21B. Nashville: Broadman and Holman, 2009.
Kletter, Raz. *The Judean Pillar-Figurines and the Archaeology of Asherah*. British Archaeological Reports International Series 636. London: Tempus Reparatum, 1996.
La Croix, Richard R. "Augustine on the Simplicity of God." *The New Scholasticism* 51 (1977) 453–69.
Lamont, John. "Aquinas on Divine Simplicity." *Monist* 80 (1997) 521–38.
Lawson, John. *The Biblical Theology of Saint Irenaeus*. London: Epworth, 1948.
Leftow, Brian. "Divine Simplicity." *Faith and Philosophy* 23 (2006) 365–80.
———. "Is God an Abstract Object?" *Nous* 24 (1990) 581–98.
———. "The Roots of Eternity." *Religious Studies* 24 (1988) 189–212.
Leithart, Peter J. *Athanasius*. Grand Rapids: Baker, 2011.
Lincoln, Andrew T. *Ephesians*. Word Biblical Commentary 42. Dallas: Word, 1990.
Longenecker, Richard N. *Galatians*. Word Biblical Commentary 41. Dallas: Word, 1990.
Lonergan, Bernard. *The Triune God: Systematics*. Toronto: University of Toronto Press, 2009.

Mann, William E. "Divine Simplicity." *Religious Studies* 18 (1982) 451–71.

———. "Simplicity and Immutability in God." *International Philosophical Quarterly* 23 (1983) 267–76.

———. "Simplicity and Properties: A Reply to Morris." *Religious Studies* 22 (1986) 343–53.

Marenbon, John. *Boethius*. Oxford: Oxford University Press, 2003.

Marshall, I. Howard. *The Pastoral Epistles*. The International Critical Commentary. Edinburgh: T. & T. Clark, 2004.

Martin, C. B. "God, the Null Set and Divine Simplicity." In *The Challenge to Religion Today*, edited by John King-Farlow, 138–43. New York: Science History, 1976.

Mascall, Eric L. *He Who Is: A Study in Traditional Theism*. London: Longmans, Green and Company, 1943.

May, James Luther. *Psalms*. Interpretation. Louisville: John Knox, 1994.

McBride, S. Dean. "The Yoke of the Kingdom: An Exposition of Deuteronomy 6:4–5." *Interpretation* 27 (1973) 273–306.

McCracken, George E. *Arnobius of Sicca: The Case against the Pagans: Books 1–3*. Ancient Christian Writers 7. Westminster, Maryland: Newman, 1949.

Meijer, P. A. *Plotinus on the Good or the One (Enneads VI, 9): An Analytical Commentary*. Amsterdam Classical Monographs 1. Amsterdam: Gieben, 1992.

Meredith, Anthony. *Gregory of Nyssa*. New York: Routledge, 1999.

Meyers, Carol L., and Eric M. Meyers. *Zechariah 9–14*. Anchor Yale Bible 25C. New Haven: Yale University Press, 1998.

Miller, Barry. *A Most Unlikely God*. Notre Dame: University of Notre Dame Press, 1996.

———. "On 'Divine Simplicity: A New Defense.'" *Faith and Philosophy* 11 (1994) 474–77.

Minns, Denis. *Irenaeus: An Introduction*. London: T. & T. Clark, 2010.

Moo, Douglas J. *James*. Tyndale New Testament Commentaries. Grand Rapids: Eerdmans, 1985.

Moreland, James P., and William L. Craig. *Philosophical Foundations for a Christian Worldview*. Downers Grove, IL: InterVarsity, 2003.

Morreall, John. *Analogy and Talking about God: A Critique of the Thomistic Approach*. Washington, DC: University Press of America, 1979.

———. "Divine Simplicity and Divine Properties." *The Journal of Critical Analysis* 7 (1978) 67–70.

Morris, Thomas V. "Dependence and Divine Simplicity." *International Journal for Philosophy of Religion* 23 (1988) 161–74.

———. "God and the World: A Look at Process Theology." In *Anselmian Explorations: Essays in Philosophical Theology*, 124–50. Notre Dame, IN: University of Notre Dame Press, 1987.

———. "On God and Mann: A View of Divine Simplicity." *Religious Studies* 21 (1985) 299–318.

———. *Our Idea of God*. Vancouver: Regent College, 1991.

Mullins, Ryan T. "Simply Impossible: A Case against Divine Simplicity." Forthcoming in *The Journal of Reformed Theology*. Online: http://www.academia.edu/572124/Something_Much_Too_Radical_To_Believe_Towards_a_Refutation_of_Divine_Simplicity.

Nash-Marshall, Siobhan. "God, Simplicity, and the *Consolatio Philosophiae*." *American Catholic Philosophical Quarterly* 78 (2005) 225–46.

O'Brien, Peter T. *Ephesians*. Pillar New Testament Commentary. Grand Rapids: Eerdmans, 1999.

Bibliography

Oden, Thomas C. *The Living God: Systematic Theology: Volume One.* San Francisco: Harper and Row, 1987.
Oliphint, K. Scot. *Reasons for Faith.* Philipsburg, NJ: Presbyterian & Reformed, 2006.
Olyan, Saul. *Asherah and the Cult of YHWH in Israel.* Atlanta: Scholars, 1988.
O'Meara, John J. *Understanding Augustine.* Portland, OR: Four Courts, 1997.
Oppy, Graham. "The Devlish Complexities of Divine Simplicity." *Philo* 6 (2003) 10–22.
Osborn, Eric F. *Irenaeus of Lyons.* Cambridge: Cambridge University Press, 2001.
———. *Justin Martyr.* Tübingen: Mohr-Siebeck, 1973.
———. *The Philosophy of Clement of Alexandria.* Cambridge: Cambridge University Press, 1957.
———. *Tertullian: First Theologian of the West.* Cambridge: Cambridge University Press, 1997.
Oswalt, John N. *Isaiah 40–66.* The New International Commentary on the Old Testament. Grand Rapids: Eerdmans, 1998.
Patai, Raphael. *The Hebrew Goddess.* 3rd ed. Detroit: Wayne State University, 1990.
Patterson, Robert L. *The Concept of God in the Philosophy of Aquinas.* London: Allen & Unwin, 1933.
Petersen, David L. *Zechariah 9–14 and Malachi.* Louisville: Westminster John Knox, 1995.
Plantinga, Alvin. *Does God Have a Nature?* Milwaukee: Marquette University Press, 1980.
Radde-Gallwitz, Andrew. *Basil of Caesarea, Gregory of Nyssa, and the Transformation of Divine Simplicity.* New York: Oxford University Press, 2009.
Rankin, David. *Athenagoras: Philosopher and Theologian.* Farnham, UK: Ashgate, 2009.
Richards, Jay Wesley. *The Untamed God.* Downers Grove, IL: InterVarsity, 2003.
Richardson, Kurt A. *James.* New American Commentary 36. Nashville: Broadman and Holman, 1997.
Rogers, Katherin. "The Traditional Doctrine of Divine Simplicity." *Religious Studies* 32 (1996) 165–86.
Rogers, Rick. *Theophilus of Antioch: The Life and Thought of a Second-Century Bishop.* Lanham, MD: Lexington, 2000.
Ross, James. "Comments on 'Absolute Simplicity'." *Faith and Philosophy* 2 (1985) 383–90.
Runia, David T. *Philo of Alexandria, On the Creation of the Cosmos according to Moses.* Philo of Alexandria Commentary Series V. 1. Leiden: Brill, 2001.
Sadler, Mark D. *Simply Divine: Simplicity as Fundamental to the Nature of God.* PhD diss., Southwestern Baptist Theological Seminary, 2004.
Schleiermacher, Friedrich. *The Christian Faith.* Philadelphia: Fortress, 1976.
Schmitt, Yann. "The Deadlock of Absolute Divine Simplicity." *International Journal for Philosophy of Religion* 74 (2013) 117–30.
Shedd, William G. T. *Dogmatic Theology.* 2 vols. New York: Scribner's Sons, 1888.
Smith, Barry D. *The Indescribable God: Divine Otherness in Christian Theology.* Eugene, OR: Pickwick, 2012.
Smith, Gary V. *Isaiah 40–66.* The New American Commentary 15b. Nashville: Broadman and Holman, 2009.
Smith, Mark S. *The Early History of God: YHWH and the Other Deities in Ancient Israel.* San Francisco: Harper & Row, 1990.
Sokolowski, Robert. *The God of Faith and Reason.* 2nd ed. Washington, DC: The Catholic University of America Press, 1985.
Stead, Christopher. *Divine Substance.* Oxford: Oxford University Press, 1977.

Strawson, Peter F. *The Bounds of Sense: An Essay on Kant's Critique of Pure Reason.* London: Methuen, 1966.
Stump, Eleonore. *Aquinas.* Arguments of the Philosophers. New York: Routledge, 2003.
Stump, Eleonore, and Norman Kretzmann. "Absolute Simplicity." *Faith and Philosophy* 2 (1985) 353–81.
Swinburne, Richard. *The Christian God.* Oxford: Clarendon, 1994.
Tate, Marvin E. *Psalms 51–100.* Word Biblical Commentary 20. Dallas: Word, 1990.
Teske, Roland J. "Properties of God and the Predicaments in *De Trinitate* V." *The Modern Schoolman* 59 (1981) 1–19.
Thompson, J. A. *Jeremiah.* The New International Commentary on the Old Testament. Grand Rapids: Eerdmans, 1980.
Toorn, Karel van der. "Goddesses in Early Israelite Religion." In *Ancient Goddesses: The Myths and the Evidence*, edited by L. Goodison and C. Morris, 83–97. Madison, WI: University of Wisconsin, 1998.
Vaggione, Richard P. *Eunomius of Cyzicus and the Nicene Revolution.* New York: Oxford University Press, 2000.
Vallicella, William F. "Divine Simplicity: A New Defense." *Faith and Philosophy* 9 (1992) 508–25.
———. "Divine Simplicity." In *The Stanford Encyclopedia of Philosophy*, Fall 2010 Edition, edited by Edward N. Zalta. Online: http://plato.stanford.edu/archives/fall2010/entries/divine-simplicity/
———. "On Property Self-Exemplification: Rejoinder to Miller." *Faith and Philosophy* 11 (1994) 478–81.
Visser, Sandra and Williams, Thomas. *Anselm.* New York: Oxford University Press, 2009.
Wainwright, William J. "Augustine on God's Simplicity: A Reply." *New Scholasticism* 53 (1979) 124–27.
———. "God's Body." In *The Concept of God*, edited by Thomas V. Morris, 72–87. Oxford: Oxford University Press, 1974.
Waltke, Bruce K., and Michael P. O'Connor. *An Introduction to Biblical Hebrew Syntax.* Winona Lake, IN: Eisenbrauns, 1990.
Ward, Keith. *The Concept of God.* Oxford: Blackwell, 1974.
Waszink, J. H., and J. C. M. van Winden. *Tertullianus De Idolatria. Critical Text and Commentary.* Supplements to Vigiliane Christianae 1. Leiden: Brill, 1987.
Way, Sr Agnes Clare, C.D.P., translator. *St. Basil: Letters: vol. 1.* The Fathers of the Church, volume XIII. Washington, DC: Catholic Universities of America Press, 1951.
Weedman, Mark. *The Trinitarian Theology of Hilary of Poitiers.* Supplements to Vigiliae Christianae 89. Leiden: Brill, 2007.
Weigel, Peter. *Aquinas on Simplicity.* Bern: Lang, 2008.
Weinandy, Thomas G. *Athanasius: A Theological Introduction.* Aldershot, UK: Ashgate, 2007.
Weiser, Artur. *The Psalms: A Commentary.* The Old Testament Library. Philadelphia: Westminster John Knox, 1962.
Westermann, Claus. *Isaiah 40–66.* The Old Testament Library. London: SCM, 1969.
Whittaker, John. "Ἄρρητος καὶ ἀκατονόματος." In *Platonismus und Christentum: Festschrift für Heinrich Dörrie*, edited by Horst-Dieter Blume und Friedhelm Mann, 303–6. Jahrbuch für Antike und Christentum, Ergänzungsband 10. Münster: Aschendorff, 1983.
———. "Ammonius on the Dephic E." *The Classical Quarterly* 19 (1969) 185–92.

Bibliography

———. "Philological Comments on the Neoplatonic Notion of Infinity." In *The Significance of Neoplatonism*, edited by R. Baines Harris, 155–72. Studies in Neoplatonism 1. Norfolk, VA: International Society for Neoplatonic Studies, 1976.

Wierenga, Edward. *The Nature of God*. Ithaca, NY: Cornell University Press, 1989.

Williams, C. J. F. *What is Existence?* Clarendon Library of Logic and Philosophy. Oxford: Oxford University Press, 1981.

Williams, D. C. "On the Elements of Being: I." *Review of Metaphysics* 7 (1953) 3–18.

———. "On the Elements of Being: II." *Review of Metaphysics* 7 (1953) 171–92.

Winston, David. "Philo's Conception of the Divine Nature." In *Neoplatonism and Jewish Thought*, edited by Lenn E. Goodman, 21–42. Studies in Neo-Platonism, Ancient and Modern 7. Albany, NY: State University of New York Press, 1992.

Witherington, Ben. *1 and 2 Thessalonians: A Socio-Rhetorical Commentary*. Grand Rapids: Eerdmans, 2006.

Wolfson, Harry A. *Philo: Foundations of Religious Philosophy in Judaism, Christianity and Islam*. 2 vols. Cambridge: Harvard University Press, 1947.

Wolterstorff, Nicholas. "Divine Simplicity." In *Our Knowledge of God*, edited by Kelly James Clark, 133–49. Studies in Philosophy and Religion 16. Dordrecht: Kluwer Academic, 1992.

Zeller, Eduard. *Grundriss der Geschichte der Griechischen Philosophie*. 2nd ed. Leipzig: Fues's Verlag, 1886.

www.ingramcontent.com/pod-product-compliance
Lightning Source LLC
Chambersburg PA
CBHW070911160426
43193CB00011B/1432